# Life Is Great!

Live _YOUR_ life!

# Life Is Great!

### 7 Guidelines
### for achieving the
### life of your dreams

BY

## Dan Pliszka

even if your boat flips over

Author photo by Christopher Record

ISBN  978-0-9961884-4-9
Library of Congress Control Number:  2018962981

Published by Lorimer Press
Davidson, NC

Printed in the U.S.A.

*To Molly, my amazing wife, for her ever-positive attitude*
*and Job-like patience when I lost mine. For all of her suggestions*
*and ideas throughout this project and our life together.*
*I love you more than you will ever know.*

*For the late Maggie Jo, our beloved cocker spaniel*
*who slept at my feet while I wrote.*

*For my parents, Walter and Esther Pliszka*
*who helped me form the guidelines by which I have lived my life.*

# TABLE OF CONTENTS

# INTRODUCTION

This book is about designing and living the life of your dreams. But what does the "life of your dreams" mean?

Today, unfortunately, when someone says, "I'm living the dream" it's often said with sarcasm and we infer that the individual is doing exactly the opposite, that they are enduring the drudgery of their existence with no goal other than to make it through the day.

To me, living the life of your dreams means pursuing the things that inspire and excite you. When you are truly living the life of your dreams, you end each day feeling fulfilled and complete. You're excited for tomorrow.

• • •

The title of this book is a metaphor for taking chances. After I'd owned a motorcycle, a sports car, and jumped from an airplane, my mother should have been used to hearing exciting news during our weekly phone calls. The day I bought my first boat, I called her, excited to tell her about my latest acquisition.

However, the first thing she said was, "What happens if the boat flips over?"

All I could say was, "Well, I guess I'll get wet."

That day, talking on the phone with my mom, I knew that if my new boat flipped over, it would be because I had done something stupid, or I was out on the lake in weather totally unsuited for boating. In either of those cases, shame on me. Otherwise, I envisioned countless, fun-filled days floating on the huge lake that was right in my backyard.

I'm writing this book to let you know that if you want to do something—as long as it isn't illegal or immoral—by all means do it!

But know that living your dreams isn't always easy. You must be prepared for others to second guess your decisions. And you must be prepared to ignore those nay-sayers—no matter how much they love you, no matter how much they want to protect you.

I should have anticipated my mom's response, she was the type of person who shied away from risk. I, on the other hand, sought it out. I've built my life around taking risks—calculated ones. My professional career has been in risk management. And in my personal life, by understanding risk and taking risks I've enjoyed a full and rich life—in other words, the life of my dreams.

That's what I want for you. I want you to expect the best, and be prepared for opposition.

It takes courage and commitment to pursue the life of your

dreams. There will be struggles, roadblocks, and set-backs. There will also be sweet victories.

I've had good teachers and bad; I've been married and divorced and married again. I've had good jobs and bad; hired for positions I sought but not hired for others. I have acquired material possessions that I desired while others still remain beyond my reach.

I haven't done everything I want to and likely never will. I have plenty of dreams left in my hopper and I hope my hopper will never be empty. I believe the best is yet to come.

I am "living the dream" and I wrote this book to document how I managed to do it. In doing so, it is my hope that I can help you achieve the life of *your* dreams.

What does the life of your dreams look like?

Is it a life of happiness and contentment? Is it to be ultra-wealthy? Is it to have a houseful of kids?

Only you can answer those questions. Let's get started!

# Forget the Rules 1

I HAVE THOUGHT A LOT about what the building blocks of the ideal life might be. Unlike constructing a house, there isn't a step-by-step guide to creating the life of your dreams. In fact, no one ever succeeds at building the *perfect* life, and most of us will end up with some unfinished business and more than a few regrets.

None of us arrived here with an owner's manual and as a result we write the manual as we go along. Most of us learn lessons the hard way. If we only had a guidebook, then we would recognize the road markers and heed the maintenance tips. We'd be headed in the right direction and life would run more smoothly.

## LIFE IS AN ADVENTURE

Living the life of your dreams is a little like taking a cross-country road trip. On such a journey, it's impossible to be 100% on target, 100% of the time.

Accept from the start that there will be times that you won't be on course. (Sometimes you might veer way off course.) Don't let that get you down. You may take a few wrong turns. There may be construction. You might face foul weather. You could have car trouble.

In addition to encountering obstacles, having to make choices further complicates your travel.

Northern route or southern? Your car or a rental? Interstate highways or back roads? Strict time schedule or a more leisurely one? Travel by day, night, or both? Follow the speed limit, or take a chance? Chain motels, bed and breakfasts, camping, or driving straight-through?

The choices are yours to make.

Unless you are really adventurous—or borderline reckless—you wouldn't set out to travel across the country without some kind of plan.

Our lives are full of choices and obstacles—many more than we encounter on a road trip. Why is it then that so many of us are living day to day without any plan in place? Think about it. Many people go about the task of living without a thought as to where they are going or even why they are going there.

How do they even know if they arrive at their destination? Life, far more complex and critical than any cross-country road trip, requires a plan.

## How Did I Get Here?

I can say at this point in my life, I've done pretty well. I've achieved many of my goals.

Did I follow a plan?

Yes, I had a plan, but it wasn't devised in an expertly orchestrated or extremely methodical manner.

Years ago, I attended a risk management conference where Susan O'Malley, the former President of Washington Sports and Entertainment and the first female president of a professional sports franchise, delivered the keynote address.

O'Malley began her career as an intern for the Washington Bullets (now the Wizards) in the National Basketball Association and rose to the position of president before she was 30 years old. Her accomplishments were certainly impressive and I hung on her every word.

During her speech, she shared her famous Seven Rules. I wrote all of them down on my note pad. Her message stuck.

She convinced me that if I followed these rules I would be happy and successful. Conversely, I knew that my life would be tougher and far less enjoyable if I didn't.

After the conference, I returned to my office and typed up O'Malley's Seven Rules. I framed them. I told my staff about them. I encouraged everyone I knew to follow them.

### O'MALLEY'S SEVEN RULES

1. Make your bed everyday.
2. Plan your work and work your plan.
3. Outwork everybody, everyday.
4. Set expectations.
5. When you mess up, make it right.
6. Do the right thing, even when no one is looking.
7. Have fun—make work fun.

Those rules look pretty good, don't they? I thought so, too, until I found myself in a "do as I say, not as I do" mode with my staff. It seemed that O'Malley's rules didn't quite fit my lifestyle. For a long time, I couldn't figure out why. Then it finally dawned on me.

I don't like rules.

Rules have the tendency to be rigid and I don't like rigidity. Of course society requires that we follow certain rules: we should not steal, assault, or kill. And I can't just move into my neighbor's house just because I like it better than mine.

There is a lot to admire in O'Malley's Rules and I'm not discounting them, but because they were rules, I chafed against them. Rules seemed inflexible.

I needed something else to model my life around; something that sounded a little more forgiving. Something that allowed for versatility. I knew there would be times I might need to break, or at least bend, the rules. There would be times when I needed to add to the list. Other times, I might need to subtract. I would never feel comfortable with something as hard and fast as "rules."

Then it came to me like a ray of sun shining through a thunderous sky.

*Guideline.*

A guideline was something I could live with and live by.

I found that pursuing the life of my dreams could be accomplished by following guidelines. By following guidelines rather than rules, I could work within certain parameters, consider recommendations, weigh suggestions, seek advice—rather than adhere to unyielding rules and regulations. In hindsight, I now realize I've followed a few basic guidelines.

## PLISZKA'S SEVEN GUIDELINES

1. Take control.
2. Believe you can!
3. Be BOLD!
4. Find your values.
5. Realize that everyone is smarter than you.
6. Know that life is too short.
7. HAVE FUN!

In the next chapters you will find a nugget (or seven) that will help you devise the right plan to realize the life of *your* dreams.

# Take Control **2**

REGARDLESS WHERE YOU are right now, you can do anything you want. The only thing between you and an
extraordinary life is you. You may not realize it, but
you are in the driver's seat of your life. In other words, you're
in control.

If you don't feel as if you are the driving force in your life,
then it might be time to conduct a life audit. This will help you
identify those aspects in your life that are going well, while also
looking at what might be missing or needs improvement.

The exercise is not a detailed analysis of your past. Rather,
it is a tool that helps evaluate your present and set your course
for the future.

To conduct your life audit, reserve a block of private time

of at least an hour, though it may take several hours, over the course of several days.

Find a place where you can sit in quiet reflection. Get out a sheet of paper, or better yet, use a notebook, or a bound journal so you can keep your audit in a safe place and refer to it later. For those so inclined, set up a file on your computer. A computerized version might provide a little more security and privacy. (Consider password protecting your work.)

On the first page, create a list of all the aspects of your life. Be sure to include things that are going well and those that are not. The following is a list to get you started. Feel free to add or subtract from it as you see fit.

## LIFE AUDIT TOPICS
- Career
- Financial Stability
- Education
- Health
- Personal Relationships
- Societal Connections
- Social and Leisure Activities
- Spiritual/Metaphysical Connections
- Children/Parents

Number your list of audit topics in order, from those you feel are going the best to those that need most improvement.

On the second page, create an audit tree by writing your top "going best" aspect on top of the page. Draw a line down the middle of the page and label one column "Going Well" and the other "Needs Improvement."

LIFE ASPECT:

| Going Well | Needs Improvement |
| --- | --- |
| | |

Make a sheet for each aspect on your list. As you evaluate each topic, think carefully about where you are succeeding as well as how you might improve. Evaluate each category as candidly as possible. You owe yourself honesty and thoroughness.

As you complete your audit pages, consider asking these questions:

- What do I like best about _____?
- What do I like least about _____?
- Am I good at _____?
- Do I procrastinate doing things with _____?
- Am I proud of how I do _____?
- What makes me good at _____?

- If I'm not good at _____, what would it take to get better?
- Is _____ in balance?
- If _____ is out of balance, why?
- Do I know someone who I consider to be good at _____? Why are they good at _____?
- Has _____ gotten better or worse over time?
- Has _____ ever been good and when?
- What about _____ was different when it was good, or needs to be different to become better?

As you review each page, evidence of where you are succeeding or failing shows up when there is a preponderance of comments in one column or the other.

On each sheet, draw a line across the bottom of the sheet numbering 10 on the left to 1 on the right. Now, review your sheet, and after careful thought, circle the number that corresponds to how you rank this life aspect.

Anything that you rank as a 10 means this part of your life is going very well. A rank of less than 10 indicates some room for improvement.

You may discover that your life is going better than you first thought. Or you might realize you have some work to do.

*There are three things hard:*
*steel,*
*a diamond,*
*and to know one's self.*

—Benjamin Franklin

## AVA

Ava conducted a life audit early in her career. The following are her "relationship" and "career" sheets.

### LIFE ASPECT: RELATIONSHIP

| Going Well | Needs Improvement |
|---|---|
| My partner is my best friend | I wish my partner were not so messy |
| We share similar values & views on important issues | I wish my partner liked "everything" on their pizza instead of just pepperoni. |
| We have a strong & loving relationship | |
| We are financially secure | |

10    ⑨    8    7    6    5    4    3    2    1

Looking at these two aspects of Ava's audit, it is clear that her relationship is going quite well. Her "going well" column certainly outweighs the "needs improvement" column.

## LIFE ASPECT: CAREER

| Going Well | Needs Improvement |
|---|---|
| I have a strong background in accounts payable & receivable. | I don't have professional credentials, designations, or certifications that would help advance my career |
| I have an advanced degree that will help get my foot in the door | I don't have experience with the budget process |
| I have five years' experience as an accountant | I don't have experience with complex finance and bond issuance |
| | I lack experience with business strategies |
| | I don't have a strong professional network |

10  9  8  7  6  5  ④  3  2  1

However, Ava's life audit demonstrated that her career deserved attention. Though she was at the beginning stages of her career, she had a long-term goal of becoming a Chief Financial Officer (CFO). Her audit tree revealed some issues she had to address before she could reach her goal.

• • •

Now review your "going well" columns and select five statements that are most significant to you. List them on a separate piece of paper. Next, review your "needs improvement" columns and pick five things you would most like to improve. Write those down on another piece of paper.

You now have two lists.

The first one is your gratitude list. Stop and take time to reflect on those things that are going well. Celebrate the fact that certain aspects in your life are going well. Thank the people who have helped make this possible.

The second list is the beginning of your future. Don't just file it away! This is the road map to reaching the destination you desire.

## TIME TO GET REAL

Even though you think you were completely honest during your life audit, there is a chance that blind spots may have led you to over- or underestimate your current situation. Sharing the results of your audit with someone who knows you well— a spouse, significant other, or close friend, will give you a clearer perspective.

Let your reality check partner know that you are on a journey of personal improvement and ask her to be part of your plan. Ask for candid and honest feedback with the stipulation that she abstain from passing any judgment on how you completed your audit.

The role of the reality check partner is two-fold: First, this person will point out where you may have erred in self-evaluation. Second, she should help you brainstorm what actions you should take next. She might help define solutions to existing problems, and identify the obstacles you might face as you move forward.

## THE BIG WHY

The life audit helps you identify where your life stands. Once you know where you stand, the next step is to define a reason for action.

Without knowing the purpose behind your goals, it is sometimes difficult to move forward. For instance, if you think you might want to pursue a degree, you might question the value of further education. When you identify the link between what you want to do and where you want to go, you are more motivated. Once you see that learning new skills will allow you to advance your career, you're more likely to enroll in the necessary classes.

Gary Keller writes in *The Millionaire Real Estate Agent*, "… one thing that all high achievers have in common is they are working for a Big Why. The Big Why is about having purpose, a mission, or a need, that in turn gives you focus. High achievers always have a Big Why powering their actions."

Suppose you are asked to put together a presentation for your company's board of directors. If you ask why and your boss says, "Because I said so!" your level of motivation might be lower than if he says, "If you 'nail' this presentation, the board will probably make a significant capital investment and you will get a 50% raise."

Knowing *why* you're doing something directly influences its importance.

My editor helped me establish the Big Why for this book. We were going over some edits and she asked me rather candidly, "Why are you writing this book?" My first answer was "I've always wanted to write a book." She looked at me as if that answer wasn't good enough and I knew it wasn't.

Not having a clear answer bothered me. The next day, it hit me—I was writing this book because one of my missions is to change the world. I hope to do this by engaging people in dialogues that change thoughts and actions that result in the betterment of life.

I have yet to see if I will accomplish my mission, but defining my Big Why helped me stay on target and finish the project.

## SANDY

After completing her life audit, Sandy realized that it was time to improve her health and become more height/weight proportionate. When her reality check partner asked why, Sandy listed these reasons:

- Because I want to.

- My clothes don't fit well and I have a closet full of clothes that would fit if I just lost some weight.

- My doctor told me that my high blood pressure and elevated blood sugar will eventually cause more serious health concerns in the future and it could possibly shorten my life and I don't want to die.

- I have two young children. I want to be a good example for them so they can live a long and healthy life and at the same time, I will be able to live longer in order to watch them grow, prosper, and perhaps have children of their own.

• My tennis game is really progressing well and if I were
in better shape and a little lighter, I might be able to
progress even further.

Which of Sandy's answers points to her Big Why? The first
one, "Because I want to," might be enough to motivate her to
action, but it probably isn't her Big Why. Not wanting to die is
a good reason to change; not wanting to die in order to be with
her children was her Big Why.

In determining your Big Why, you will most likely find it
is driven by a host of smaller whys.

After defining your Big Why, it's time to map out what you
need to do to reach your destination.

Here's where you refer back to your life audit lists and the
conversations you had with your reality check partner.

## That Four-Letter Word: PLAN

Remember Ava? After completing her life audit, she stated her
desire to become a CFO. Her quest to achieve this goal can't
end there. What comes next? Ideally, she would review her life
audit and prioritize the list of things that needed improvement
with regards to her career. If she made credentialing her top pri-

*If you fail to plan,*
*you are planning to fail.*

—Benjamin Franklin

ority she might decide to become a Certified Public Accountant (CPA). That might lead her to ask the following questions:

- What education is required to become a CPA?
- What are the requirements for taking the CPA exam?
- What experience must I have before becoming a CPA?
- How do I become a licensed CPA in my state?
- How do I qualify for interstate and international reciprocity certificates?
- Once certified, what is required to maintain certification?

The answers to these questions are the foundation of Ava's intermediate plan—becoming a CPA—which will in turn pave the way to her becoming a CFO.

It's time for you to look at the list of things that you identified as needing improvement. Once you've identified your reasons for *why* you want to improve, i.e., your motivation, you'll be ready to pursue some goals.

## Setting Goals

Anyone who has done even a little bit of research on goal setting has come across something called S.M.A.R.T. goals. Introduced by George T. Doran, a consultant and former Director of Corporate Planning for Washington Water Power Company, the acronym S.M.A.R.T. stands for: Specific, Measurable, Assignable, Realistic, and Time-related. S.M.A.R.T. goals can be used in almost any setting. They help manage expectations related to completing objectives. For instance, this morning, I set two goals for myself.

The first was to finish editing this chapter today. The second goal for the day was to clean and organize the workshop in my garage. Take a look at cleaning and organizing my shop and see if it is a S.M.A.R.T. goal. Is it:

- **SPECIFIC?** Yes. To clean and organize the workshop.
- **MEASURABLE?** Yes. Everything will be stored in its appropriate place and all surfaces will be clutter and debris free.
- **ASSIGNABLE?** Yes. I'm the man for the job.
- **REALISTIC?** Yes. It can be done, but if you've seen my shop lately....
- **TIME-BOUND?** Yes. I will begin at noon and finish by dinnertime today.

Just setting a S.M.A.R.T. goal for yourself doesn't guarantee you will complete it. Truth be known, editing this chapter took much longer than I expected. When noon rolled around I was still at my desk, not in my garage.

Goals—sometimes we set them, and sometimes we miss them.

Depending on the magnitude and consequence of any specific goal, missing your completion target by an hour, a day, or even a week might not matter.

I underestimated the time it would take to edit this chapter and editing was my highest priority. I had no shop project planned, so if my garage remained disorganized and dirty another week or two, it wouldn't matter. Still, it bugs me that my garage is a mess.

In other cases, though, a goal can have a "drop dead" deadline that must be met—or else.

For example, a salesperson responding to a request for proposals is usually given an absolute deadline with a specific date, time, and place where the proposal must be delivered. If he misses that deadline by even a second, he may miss out on winning that particular piece of business.

Most life goals don't have such exacting deadlines. Consequently we have some flexibility in completing them. While allowing some slack is okay, all too often we repeatedly miss self-imposed deadlines and then totally fail to reach our goals.

## Our Biggest Enemy

While there are many reasons for failing to achieve goals, procrastination is the reason that most often rears its ugly head.

Merriam-Webster defines procrastination as "intentionally and habitually putting off something that should be done."

A Google search for "causes of procrastination" brings up

more than three million results! The most common reasons we procrastinate are:

- Fear
- Lack of Purpose or Direction
- Perfectionism
- Complexity

## FEAR

I've spent my entire professional career as a risk manager, and most people think my job is to fear everything and steer everyone away from risk. That notion can't be further from the truth.

*Everything* has an element of risk.

Risk is the uncertainty of being able to complete an objective.

My job is not to fear risk or to eliminate it entirely. Instead, I evaluate and measure risk in order to find ways around, through, or under it. My job is to assess and measure potential effects of risk; unless an activity is illegal or immoral, I rarely recommend avoiding a risk in its entirety.

Risks can be either positive or negative. If you were to invest money in a start-up business and it takes off and makes a return on investment, it's positive. If you lose money, it was obviously negative.

By not taking some measured risks, we miss out on oppor-

*The only thing
we have to fear
is fear itself.*

—Franklin D. Roosevelt,
first inaugural address

tunities. Every venture has a measure of risk. If there is no risk, there is no reward (profit) and usually, the bigger the risk, the bigger the potential reward. The converse is also true, bigger risks have a potential for a much bigger down-side.

The same goes with pursuing personal goals. Just by taking actions on the results of your life audit, you win. The win comes from seeking what you want out of life versus staying mired in unhappiness.

• • •

Perhaps one of the biggest risk takers of all time was Neil Armstrong, the first man to walk on the moon. I've often wondered if Armstrong had any fears regarding space travel and his eventual moon walk.

Any fears were likely allayed by his life-long conditioning. When he was two years old, his father took him to air races in Cleveland, Ohio. From that day on, Armstrong was fascinated with flight. When he was five years old, he took his first airplane ride. When he turned 16, before he could legally drive a car, he earned his flight certificate and made his first solo flight. From there, he became a naval aviator, test pilot, and astronaut.

He took life and death risks when he strapped himself in a capsule on top of a rocket. Of course, that ended in the reward of being the first person to walk on the moon. He took big risks, managed them, and became successful.

Contrast Armstrong with people who dream of visiting far-away places and seeing some of the wonders of the world, but who refuse to get on an airplane. Their fears severely limit their life experiences.

Why go on about why you can't do something? Instead, go out, be a little daring, and just get it done.

After the stock market crash of 1929, the country plunged into Great Depression, and people—out of work, hungry, miserable—were understandably afraid that they would not survive the economic downturn. After Franklin Delano Roosevelt became president in 1933, he took the long view.

He believed that the challenges facing the nation were common, material, and therefore solvable.

Roosevelt believed that fear was making things worse. Recognizing fear as a factor, he worked hard to reassure the public with fireside chats and New Deal initiatives that he candidly said were "bold, persistent experimentation." His plan was to "take a method and try it: if it fails, admit it frankly and try another." By confronting fear head on, F.D.R. helped lead the U.S. out of the worst economic downturn in its history.

• • •

If fear is causing you to procrastinate pursuing goals, how can you overcome that fear? Look at the following questions. By answering them you will be able to evaluate the level of risk involved in pursuing your goal. Then you can make a rational decision about whether to proceed or not.

- Do I even know if I'm afraid of something?
- What exactly am I afraid of?
- What exactly am I *not* afraid of?
- What is the worst that can happen?
- What is the best that can happen?
- Where can I get more information about my fear?
- Do we know anyone that has successfully faced this fear?
- Where did this fear come from?
- Is my fear rational and based in fact, or a myth?

Here's what happened when Sam was hesitating to ask Liza out on a first date. Using the above questions, he was able to make a rational decision about asking her out.

- What exactly are you afraid of, Sam?

  *Rejection, embarrassment, humiliation.*

- What exactly are you *not* afraid of?

  *Finding something to do or somewhere to go.*

- What is the worst that can happen?

  *She says no, embarrasses, or humiliates me.*

- What is the best that can happen?

  *She says yes, we hit it off, we have a marvelous time, and live happily ever after.*

- Where can you get more information about your fears?

  *I could talk to friends or family who can point out some of my best qualities, boost my confidence. I could talk to someone who knows Liza and learn more about her.*

- Do you know anyone who has successfully faced this fear?

  *My brother may have gone through this same thing. Come to think of it, so did my roommate in college.*

- Where did this fear come from?

  *I am shy, and I had a bad experience before.*

- Is your fear rational and based in fact, or a myth?

  *Liza seems nice. But how much do I really know about her? I probably should find out whether she is married or dating someone else.*

With this scenario, Sam saw that the worst that could happen is that Liza would say no to his invitations. With no life or death implications in the balance, Sam saw that the risk was worth taking, so he asked her out!

## LACK OF PURPOSE OR DIRECTION

Procrastination can also occur due to lack of purpose. Millennials, young adults born between 1980-2000, get a bad rap for being selfish or lazy. Not so. A study published by Harris Interactive, on behalf of the Career Advisory Board, found that: "Millennials believe 'success' is a career where they do meaningful and personally fulfilling work that has a positive impact on others or on society as a whole while earning a high salary."

Don't you want to feel as if your job and your life has a meaningful purpose? Doesn't everyone? We all want to know how we fit into this thing we call life. We want to answer the question: "What is my purpose?"

Finding your purpose may be a two-stage process: finding meaning in your work, and finding meaning in your life.

Ideally, the quest would be to find work that fulfills the meaning of your life, but that isn't always immediately possible.

My first job out of high school was working on the line in a metal forge shop. One day, I came into work and found a large bin with a big red tag marked "RUSH" at my workstation. My boss said he needed me to complete this job as fast as possible.

My boss never fully explained the reason for the rush, but I was up for the job. I believed that I was furthering the company's mission—that I was playing a role in its success.

The rush job took most of my shift to complete. When I was done, I let my boss know and he said the next shift would take care of the final steps.

Imagine my surprise when I returned to work the next day and found the bin marked RUSH still sitting at my workstation. I felt like an idiot for believing that my efforts the previous day had mattered.

This event was a wake-up call. No RUSH tags could ever convince me to work harder or faster at this job. I knew now that my work had little meaning.

Several months later, after a downturn in business, I was laid off. Losing my job forced me to face a hard truth. Since graduating from high school, I had been dragging my heels, putting off college because I had no idea where I wanted to go or what I wanted to do.

College put me on the path to a very fulfilling and meaningful line of work. For most of my career, I have helped individuals manage risks to keep them safe from harm. Ironically, I have, in many ways, kept individuals, processes, and organizations moving forward while keeping them from being paralyzed by fear.

## PERFECTIONISM

Procrastinators fall prey to setting unattainable goals and/or stringent standards. On one hand, perfectionism can be an asset for someone like a skilled surgeon who must perform at the highest level because there are dire consequences if she doesn't. On the other hand, the person who seeks perfection in everything he does may get frustrated and risks anxiety and depression. In addition, while he continues to devote unnecessary effort toward perfecting the task at hand, he missed other opportunities that he is not free to pursue.

The axiom, *If anything is worth doing, it is worth doing well,* encourages us to try our best, not seek perfection.

I've started (and never finished) somewhere around 13 different books. What stymied most of those efforts was my desire to have a perfect book when I hit print on the first draft. I spent an inordinate amount of time editing and re-editing a lot of "Chapter One"s. Reading those first chapters, when it became clear that it wasn't perfect, I became frustrated and quit.

This time around, I sought the help of a professional writer who helped me break the project into pieces. She helped me get the thoughts out of my head and onto paper. Then, together we edited, organized, and re-edited the work.

• • •

For many years, I have worked with government entities. You may have heard of the saying, "Good enough for government work" which implies the work is barely passable. However, did you know, the origin of that saying was the work was so exacting and good, it met the tough government specifications?

Anything worth doing is worth doing well; but there are limits. At some point, we need to say "good enough." Perfectionism takes too long. We waste time reaching for a level that is rarely needed. Besides that, when we stay mired in something seeking perfection, we are keeping ourselves from the next challenge.

Do your best, but don't spend too much time making it perfect.

Combine complexity with perfectionism and you have a recipe for never moving forward—complete paralysis.

## COMPLEXITY

Procrastination is most prevalent on high-stakes, unfamiliar, or complex projects. If it were easy, we'd just knock it out and be done, right?

Large and complex tasks fuel our fear of the unknown. Uncertain of the outcome and fearing failure, we become overwhelmed and delay action.

General Creighton Abrams said, "When eating an elephant, take one bite at a time." That methodology can help accomplish any goal. A nibble here and a nibble there, in a consistent and systematic way, and pretty soon you are done.

When you break a project down into smaller pieces and begin to complete the necessary tasks, you create mini-wins for yourself. Those wins help to build momentum and confidence. They will help you conquer your fear, establish your purpose, define your why, and put you on the road to success.

• • •

Armed with what you learned in the life audit, and knowing
how to break your improvement goals in to manageable pieces,
you should have a clearer idea of what is needed to begin living
the life of your dreams. Don't let the roadblocks of fear, lack of
purpose, perfectionism, or complexity interfere with your Big
Why. Resist procrastination, take some risks, dare to succeed!

Because, guess what?

You can!

*Whether you think you can,*
*or think you can't,*
*you're right.*

—Henry Ford

# You Can! 3

M Y PARENTS' MANTRA, repeated often to my siblings and me, was, "You can!" They told us we could be anything we wanted to be as long as we were the BEST at whatever it was that we chose to do. For sure, there were some unspoken caveats. Being the best bank robber in the world would have been frowned upon. Other occupations—race car driver, trapeze artist—were not forbidden per se, but they certainly didn't garner support or encouragement from Mom and Dad.

My parents not only wanted the best for their children, they wanted more for us than they'd ever had. Above all, they wanted us to be college graduates. They said a good education would always give us "something to fall back on." (They were right.)

I took my parents' mantra quite literally and believed that I could do anything I wanted. I chose to do things my way and thumbed my nose at anyone who disagreed. The world was my oyster and there were very few limits that stood between me and what I wanted to do.

While chasing my dreams, I caught some and missed some. Such is life.

Today, I want to tell you my parents' mantra is true for you, too! You can, but first you have to believe.

## BELIEVE

If you've conducted a life audit and have set some goals, you should have some inkling on what you want to accomplish. Now, you need to believe you can.

After observing many people, James Clear, blogger, author, weight lifter, and motivator, drew this conclusion about the difference between successful and unsuccessful people: "It isn't their intelligence, opportunity or resources; it is their belief that they can accomplish their goals."

The key word here is belief. *Believing* in your ability to accomplish your goal(s) is more than half the battle.

If you're ever tempted to give up and think you can't accomplish your goals, I want you to summon the image of Rob Mendez.

Born without arms or legs, Mendez coaches Junior Varsity football at Prospect High School in Saratoga, California. Eschewing prosthetics, he tools around in an electric wheelchair. He learned football by playing video games, manipulating the controller with his mouth. He says the JV job is only the beginning. At the 2019 ESPY awards, after winning the Jimmy V Award for Perseverance, he said, "When you dedicate yourself to something and open your mind to different possibilities... you really can go places in this world."

• • •

The power of belief is further illustrated by a study completed in 2002 by the Department of Veterans Affairs and Baylor College of Medicine. In the study, they took 180 patients with knee pain and broke them into 3 groups.

One group underwent arthroscopic surgery where loose and torn cartilage was cut away, and smoothed. The second group underwent a procedure where their knee joints were simply flushed out. The third group had simulated surgery where small incisions were placed around the knee area, but no instruments were inserted into the joint.

None of the patients were told which procedure they underwent, and over the next two years all three groups were followed by the researchers. All patients reported less pain and greater mobility.

The most significant finding was that no one group's results were remarkably better than another. Even though one may have expected that those who received surgical procedures would have reported better results, that was not the case. Surgery or not, patients experienced less pain.

The placebo affect improved the non-surgical patients' quality of life to the same degree

Perhaps it truly is mind over matter, and all you have to do is *BELIEVE*.


## What You Say Is What You Get

Every day during college, Tom Jones (not the singer), woke up, looked at himself in the mirror, and said, "Arise! Arise and face the challenge of the day! Tom Jones, you're so pretty—don't you ever die!"

Tom Jones was affirming that he was up to the challenges that awaited him, and by affirming that he was of great value, he helped assure his success. Further, whether he was pretty or not, by affirming to himself that he was indeed a pretty individual, that removed any need for validation from anyone else.

Both positive and negative affirmations can become true and our utterance makes them reality. Eve Hogan, in an article for *Spirituality & Health* magazine, "Affirmations: Why They Work & How to Use Them," attributes affirmations to something in our brain called the Reticular Activating System (RAS).

*If you can imagine it,*
*you can achieve it.*
*If you can dream it,*
*you can become it.*

—William Arthur Ward

The RAS is like an electrical junction box in the brain for internal mindsets and external stimuli. It has many functions, most relating to our wakefulness and alertness. It also allows us to ignore certain insignificant stimuli while remaining conscious of other stimuli.

For example, RAS allows us to ignore our nose. You may not realize this, but most of us are always viewing our nose. It's the RAS that allows us to tune out the nose and rarely notice it! If you are like most people, you probably just stopped to see if you could see your nose. It's been there all along, you just don't notice it thanks to the RAS.

The RAS is also responsible when we become aware of, or interested in, a particular model of automobile. Pretty soon, we begin to notice that model car on the road on a regular basis. The RAS is connecting our internal thoughts with the external stimuli. It's not that the cars haven't been there before, it's just that we didn't previously connect our internal thoughts with the outside stimuli.

Tom Jones used a simple affirmation to keep himself moving in a positive direction. You, too, can stay on track with your goals, aspirations by reciting affirmations on a daily basis.

Be careful though. Stay positive. Your brain, and in particular, your RAS can't distinguish between positive and negative statements.

# TALK TO YOURSELF!

If you're stuck in a state of non-believing maybe it's time to change your self talk. Henry Ford said, "If you always do what you've always done, you'll always get what you've always got." Unless you change your negatives to positives, you'll get "what you've always got."

A great place to start is with the messages you send yourself. Rather than saying, "I'm not good enough" or "I don't deserve it" take a page from Tom Jones' book and tell yourself how awesome you are.

Remember, if you maintain negative thoughts, that pesky RAS will keep your negative perceptions activated, making progress difficult.

There is no magic in creating affirmations. The important thing is to create a system that works for you, and a system that can become part of your daily routine.

Take a mental inventory of any negative self-talk you might be engaged in. Maybe you should revisit your "needs improvement" list to help recognize these.

Now, on a piece of paper DO NOT write down any of your identified negative self-talk. Rather, write down the exact opposite. If you've been telling yourself you don't deserve the best, write down that you DO deserve the best.

Write short, positive statements about the things you desire and those things that will improve your life. Keep the list simple, but comprehensive. You should be able to read your list aloud in a minute or two.

Over the next few weeks, read your list to yourself in a convincing manner every day. Read your list out loud while looking in a mirror. Be demonstrative.

Repetition is the key to changing habits; repetition helps your RAS activate and make those affirmations come to life. Define, refine, and edit your affirmations as you say them to better fit who you are and who you want to be. Continue repeating your affirmations at least once every day.

One of my affirmations is "The difference between where I am and where I want to be is what I do." I repeat that statement to myself at least twice a day—first thing in the morning and last thing before I go to bed. That helps me stay on track and believe in myself.

Yesterday, a number of work and personal commitments had been keeping me from my writing. Today, like every other day, I read my affirmations aloud. I knew that I had a free evening that could be dedicated to this project and planned to get back to work as soon as I got home.

On my way home from work, my mind wandered as it usually does while I'm driving and I began thinking about the new boat cover I needed. I thought about stopping by the boat dealer. It was on my way home and wouldn't take much time to check on it.

When I was about 500 feet from the boat dealer's parking lot, my consciousness kicked in and I thought, "You know, this will keep you from getting to where you want to be with the book." I knew where a stop like this could lead. I'd be looking at the latest boats, accessories, and talking with the staff. A 10-minute stop could easily stretch into an hour.

And I remembered that "The difference between where I am and where I want to be is what I do."

So I thought better of checking out the new boat cover and continued home where I spent the evening writing.

This was a small thing, but a million small things add up to a million bigger things.

A small detour to the boat dealer might have seemed insignificant, but it might have completely derailed this project. My affirmations convinced me to soldier on and get to the task at hand.

## VISUALIZATION

Dr. Peter Jensen, author of *Ignite The Third Factor*, said that when it comes to nature vs. nurture, it's not either/or, it's both. Each of us is affected by nature (our heredity) as well as by nurture (our socialization and upbringing). But there's something else at work that defines our success.

As a sports psychologist, Jensen has worked with world-class athletes and has had the opportunity to observe human performance at the highest level. Consequently, he insists that individuals can make conscious choices to perform at a higher level. He calls that conscious choice "the third factor" and it comes about when there is dissatisfaction with or conflict between reality and what could be.

A gymnast Jensen knew used visualization to perfect his parallel bar routine. Each night as he went to sleep, he would practice his routine in his head. He visualized each part of the routine, from start to finish. During his mental practice, he would occasionally make a mistake and that jerked him into consciousness. The next time he was physically on the bars, those past mental mistakes made him keenly aware of the need to execute those portions with greater care.

Examples abound when it comes to athletes and perfecting their performance.

Australian psychologist Alan Richardson conducted an experiment with 3 groups of basketball players over 20 days. The first group practiced throwing free-throws 20 minutes per day. The second only threw free-throws on the first and last days. The third didn't practice their free throws at all, but visualized making the shots.

Richardson reports that the first group improved their shooting percentage by 24%, the second group showed no improvement, and the third improved by 23%—nearly identical to the players who practiced their free-throws on the court.

Visualization works.

· · ·

By combining visualization and affirmations, focusing on how you want to feel, and how you want to perform, you will soon be living the life you want to live.

But this is up to you.

You alone are the one who must take the steps toward achieving the life of your dreams.

Believe in yourself and surround yourself with others who believe in you, too.

Think positive, talk positive, and act positive.

YOU can!

*Boldness be my friend.*

—William Shakespeare

# Be Bold! 4

A T THE BEGINNING of each episode of *Star Trek*, William Shatner as Captain Kirk told us the mission of Starship Enterprise was "…to boldly go where no man has gone before." Your goals may not take you to a place where no one has ever been before, but Kirk held a key to living the life of your dreams.

That key is to go *boldly*!

To live boldly means making decisions and following through with the necessary actions to take you to your chosen destination.

Living boldly opens up more options; exercising those options ultimately leads to living the life of your dreams.

## In Search of Your Daring Spirit

The dictionary definition of bold is: "fearless before danger; showing or requiring a fearless daring spirit; or, to stand out prominently."

My daring spirit was in evidence when I chose to jump out of a perfectly good airplane at 14,000 feet for the mere thrill of knowing what it was like to skydive. For me, skydiving was bold, but not reckless. I took measures to minimize the risk; I went with an experienced diver; we used parachutes.

Others take their thrills further, like wing-walking on an airplane or deep diving in the ocean.

I am not advocating a life completely absent of fear. I'm not saying go lie down in the middle of a busy street and dare traffic to hit you. That would be reckless.

The truth is being bold for you might only be driving across town. For my mom, being bold meant ordering prime rib. It's up to you to define your limits.

Whatever you do, make them *your* limits, not someone else's. Bold may be checking something off your bucket list. Two elderly ladies from Kentucky, with a life-long desire to visit New York City, saved enough money to make the trip. They carefully researched where to stay and what to do. Once they were in New York, the hotel staff looked after them as if there were family.

Upon returning to their hotel for their last night, they had just gotten on the elevator when a man's hand reached into the elevator to keep the doors from closing. In his other hand, he had two German Shepherds tethered to short leather leashes. The trio entered the elevator, the doors closed, the man said, "SIT!" and the two women hit the floor.

The man apologized immediately, telling the women he'd meant for his dogs to sit.

The next morning, when the ladies went to check out of the hotel, they learned that their bill was already paid in full— by the dogs' owner. Being bold paid some major dividends for those daring women from Kentucky.

## BEWARE FALSE ASSUMPTIONS

Remember that nothing is really risk-free. Opting out of one thing means you run the risk of missing out on something else.

Gemma once suffered a severe headache which she attributed to becoming overheated in the summer sun. For 20 years, she believed that the least bit of summer sun would cause her to experience another severe headache.

So, when the weather was hot and sunny, and her friends and family were outdoors playing tennis, or swimming, or enjoying a picnic, Gemma was nowhere to be found.

There's no denying hot summer conditions can cause headaches. But there are a host of other causes. Maybe being in the sun had been the cause of Gemma's headache. Maybe not. Perhaps she had been slightly dehydrated, or fighting a virus, or maybe stress had triggered that headache.

Regardless, after that one experience, the summer sun had become her enemy and she avoided it at all costs.

Perhaps she should have taken a chance and tip-toed back into the sun to see if she would get another headache, kept some ibuprofen on hand, and plenty of water nearby.

Instead, rather than risk another headache, she has denied herself countless opportunities for fun in the sun with her friends and family.

For Gemma, being bold would be sitting in the sun.

What is being bold for you?

It may not be easy, but find a way to forge ahead today. Take a risk, despite your past experiences.

If we let our past define us, we can't move forward.

Go on, take some chances!

## Calculated Risks

Chesley "Sully" Sullenberger, the pilot of the 2009 "Miracle on the Hudson" flight took a chance. After flying into a flock of geese, his airplane experienced total engine failure. He was left with few choices. He was too far from the closest airport to land safely on the ground. In a split-second decision, Sullenberger took a calculated risk and successfully performed a water landing on the Hudson River.

In this case, his past experiences allowed him to save the lives of the 155 passengers on board. Sully's extensive experience and training helped him instinctively react to the situation. Further, he did not let that one incident to keep him from future flights. After being cleared in the ensuing crash investigation, he quickly went back to flying passenger aircraft and did so until his retirement, concluding a 40-year career.

• • •

There is no denying that Sir Richard Branson, founder of the Virgin group of companies, is wildly successful. For many reasons, most would not have predicted that Branson would have met with much success. He learned from an early age to be tough. Though this seems cruel now, when he was a child, his mother would drop him off in the country and make him find his way back home.

Instead of being held back by obstacles, Branson broke through them. He sought to simplify ordinary, and not so ordinary, businesses. His initial foray into the airline industry was borne out of necessity (and desire).

Once, on his way to visit his girlfriend, Branson's connecting flight in the Virgin Islands, the last flight of the day, was canceled. Determined to see his girl, he decided to charter a flight. Realizing he could not afford the fare on his own, he recruited others from the canceled flight to share the cost. They all made it to the Virgin Islands that day.

One of Branson's business mantras is "Screw it, let's do it." To that end, he says, "Just do it, have fun, be bold, challenge yourself, stand on your own feet, live the moment, value friends and family, have respect, do some good."

## STANDING ON YOUR OWN FEET

We are social creatures and we wish to fit in. Consequently, we imitate the norms of our jobs, families, and communities. We then lose our true selves in the process. Soon, we find it difficult to extract ourselves from our learned and practiced patterns. Eventually, any attempt to deviate from our patterns makes us uncomfortable. That, in turn, causes us to sidestep our true calling.

Not long after moving into my first house, the doorbell rang. When I answered, I found three neighbors (two middle-aged men and a young woman) who all belonged to an area church. They had come to share some information about their faith and their church. Always curious, I invited them in.

We enjoyed a good bit of small talk about the neighborhood, work, and life in general. Eventually, the conversation turned to religion. It was clear they were recruiting new mem-

*The past does not equal the future.*

—Tony Robbins,
motivational speaker

bers and had a well-rehearsed sales pitch. Like all good group presentations, they each had their own speaking role.

When the young woman began her part, she became noticeably uncomfortable and seemed uncertain of her message. She stumbled and stammered, finally looking to her companions asking, "Now, what am I supposed to say here?"

The visit ended soon after.

Prior to her pitch, the young woman hadn't seemed scared or shy. However, as soon as her presentation began, she became discombobulated.

Perhaps it was the fear of God; though I doubt that was the case. My diagnosis is that she wasn't convinced in her convictions and had succumbed to groupthink. Perhaps, she had not yet fully formed her own thoughts on the subject, and was not able to express them.

In time, this young church lady may have found her conviction, but that day, it was clear she did not know where she stood when it came to her faith.

If I were to guess, the young woman's assessment of that afternoon was that it had been a failure. It was not. It was a learning experience. Hopefully she developed her own message that she could clearly articulate going forward, and could stand on her own two feet.

• • •

Groupthink, what happened to the young evangelist who showed up on my doorstep, occurs when someone conforms to the homogenized thoughts, morals, or mores of a group. It can be found mostly in natural groups, such as family, work, church congregations, and social clubs. When fueled by social media and personal influencers, groupthink can keep us stymied in our quest to achieve the life of our dreams.

Because we want to fit in and be accepted, we conform to others' ideas instead of our own; we fail to examine group norms and opinions through our own filters. Before we know it, our judgements meld with those of the group, and we become an altered version of our true selves.

An example of groupthink can be found in today's American politics. Driven by the two-party political system, we are clearly and vehemently divided by the loudest voices on opposing sides of the issues. Further, we are expected to sort complex problems into only two buckets: conservative or liberal.

Truth be known, few of us are situated squarely on one side or the other. In a 2016 Gallup poll, 25% of Americans surveyed identified as liberal and 36% as conservative. The remaining 39% —the majority—identified as neither, meaning they are either smack dab in the middle, conservatively liberal, or liberally conservative.

Unfortunately, politics has morphed into a zero-sum game which produces only winners and losers. Groupthink has led

*Be yourself,*
*everyone else is taken.*

—Oscar Wilde

our government to a lack of compromise, stagnation, and a failure to move on and thrive.

Don't let groupthink do the same to you.

Think for yourself!

Be yourself.

## AUTHENTICITY

What does that mean, be yourself?

Brené Brown, in her book *The Gift of Imperfection*, says, "Authenticity is the daily practice of letting go of who we think we are supposed to be and embracing who we actually are."

Is it surprising to think that we might not be who we think we are?

We have lost touch with our true selves over the years and now exist somewhere between what we thought we wanted and what everyone else wants.

The journey begins early in life. Every time we hear, "Oh, what a good boy!" we continue the behavior that elicited the praise. When scolded, we tend to avoid the behavior that produced the criticism. It is a slow abandonment of acting on our desires and caving in to the expectations and visions of others.

It doesn't matter whether those adapted behaviors are good, bad, or otherwise.

Like one of those giant rocks that school kids paint over almost daily with birthday shout-outs and game day messages, we get "painted" many times over with others' ideas, philosophies, and sentiments. Over time, those layers of paint obliterate the boulder underneath.

In most cases, our paint was probably applied by individuals who meant us no harm, and they applied it with the best of intentions.

Other times, though, paint may have been applied by someone imposing their selfish desires on us, or worse, by a person who wanted to keep us down.

A lot of us cover ourselves in paint.

In 2018, Jeff Haden wrote "Why You Are Much Better Than You Think You Are" for *Inc.* magazine. He quoted Paul McCartney as saying, "There's a line in a song on my latest album, 'Everybody else busy doing better than me.' I still think that way. I really do think that. I have to argue with myself and think, 'That's probably not true.'"

Even though few would consider Paul McCartney unsuccessful—he has 32 Billboard #1 songs, 18 Grammy Awards, and an estimated worth of $1.2 billion—the former Beatle paints himself with some self-doubt.

• • •

Bombardment from every day messages about whom we should be—Be sexy. Be thin. Don't worry. Be happy—makes it easy to see why it is so difficult to just be who we want to be.

## Stand Out Prominently

So how do we remove the layers of false identities—chip away at the paint—and re-discover our true selves?

In part, the answer can be found back in the dictionary definition of boldness. We have to be willing to go out on a limb, to risk standing out from our peers. Here are some ways to excavate yourself from under all those layers of paint and live more boldly:

- Exhibit Healthy Skepticism

Don't accept everything at face value. Ask lots of "why" questions. Confirm for yourself what is and what isn't. Once you've proven a fact, accept it as such as move on.

- Become Self-aware

Take the opportunity to showcase your strengths and at the same time recognize your weaknesses. Ask others for feedback. Keep your ego in check when receiving accolades and try not to feel defensive when confronted with constructive criticism.

- Make Mistakes

Part of living boldly involves making mistakes. You'll experiment with what works and what doesn't. You'll discover new likes and dislikes. Try new things; don't reject something simply because it doesn't *look* like something you would enjoy. Even though you may cringe when thinking about making mistakes, you learn from them and are better for having had the experience.

- BE OUTSPOKEN

  When you are confident sharing your thoughts and emotions, you show others who you are and what you stand for. Learn to think before you speak and keep your candor in check so as not to offend.

- BE PASSIONATE

  When you have found your passion(s), pursue them with near reckless abandon. With direction and purpose, you can leverage your passions to create the life of your dreams.

• • •

As you grow into your bold, authentic self, strive to be your best self. Commit to being responsible. Philosopher Søren Kierkegaard described authenticity as "an aim for a person to face reality, make decisions, commit to them, and take responsibilities for those decisions."

That sounds pretty bold to me.

Let me warn you: while boldly pursuing your goals you will encounter some trials and tribulations. Some people, pastimes, and habits might be left behind, or at least put on hold.

People close to you may think (and say) that you're crazy.

Ignore them.

Move in the direction *you* want to go.

[A FOOTNOTE HERE: *Being bold is not a license to embrace or excuse character flaws. If you are continually receiving negative feedback that you are a recalcitrant miscreant, chances are it's true. Chalking up your evil ways to just being yourself won't lead you to the life of your dreams.*]

*Rather than love,*
*than money,*
*than fame,*
*give me truth.*

—Henry David Thoreau

# Live Your Values 5

THROUGHOUT OUR LIVES, values and needs intersect and influence each other. At birth, needs trump values because first we need to survive. To survive, above all we need to breathe, eat, sleep, and poop. Most infants receive a lot of help in this regard. Others see to it that babies survive and thrive. But our physical needs are only the first in a series of needs.

Abraham Maslow at first theorized that people share five common needs:

1. PHYSICAL: food, water, rest, and warmth
2. SAFETY: security and safety
3. ACCEPTANCE AND LOVE: intimate relationships and friends
4. ESTEEM: prestige and feeling of accomplishment

5. SELF-ACTUALIZATION: achieving one's full potential

Later in his life, Maslow added one more:

6. SELF-TRANSCENDENCE

According to Maslow, when these six needs are met, not only can we survive, but we can thrive and live the life of our dreams.

While the first four criteria on Maslow's list are self-explanatory, the last two require some explanation. American psychologist, Carl Rogers, described self-actualization as man's ability to "become his potentialities." An example might be the high school basketball star who dreams of playing pro basketball and eventually finds himself living that dream. Maslow's concept of transcendence kicks in when that basketball player's "peak experiences" connect him to the cosmos.

Self-transcendence is self-actualization at the next level; the self-actualized person becomes one with the activity in which he is participating. The pro basketball player may call this being in "the zone." Not only is he doing what he has always dreamed of doing, he is doing it with such aplomb that it seems magical or supernatural.

• • •

This is where I believe our needs and values begin to intertwine. To meet our needs at the highest two levels, we need to make sure our aspirational needs are congruent with our values.

Unfortunately, our needs and values often conflict. In the highest levels of actualization, if we're not living our values, we can't meet our needs. When your life matches your values, life is harmonious. When they don't, you might feel uneasy, irritable, and powerless. At the very least, you will be stressed.

## DEFINING VALUES

Because you develop values over time, you are often unconscious to what they actually are. According to sociologist Morris Massey, values are developed in three stages. The imprint stage, from birth to about age seven, is when we accept almost all things presented to us as infallible truth. From age 8 until 13 we enter the modelling stage where we no longer blindly accept various values; rather, we try them out for ourselves. Then, in the socialization stage, from age 14 to about 21, we are largely influenced by our peers.

Whether or not you are aware of your values, they guide your behavior in everyday life. Thus, it is important to identify, know, and understand your own values. To do so will bring clarity and direction.

Unless you are at peace and content with yourself and your life, there is a good chance your values are out of alignment. If that is the case, don't worry, you are not alone. Many of us go through life misaligned because we never define and focus on our core values.

Defining core values can be confusing because the words values, ethics, and morals are somewhat interchangeable. They are transposable because there is a fine line between their meanings. For example, honesty can be a value, an ethic, and a moral.

When values, ethics, and morals are used interchangeably, they are used to describe our overall sense of right and wrong. Those values should always run in your background, much like the computer operating system that enables our computers to perform their magic.

Actually, an overall sense of right and wrong can also be a core value, depending on the individual. Think about a police officer who is truly in the job to combat society's ills. He/she may hold a strong sense of right and wrong as a core value. Conversely, a police officer who is in the job purely to control others may have control as one of his key values.

Values develop unconsciously through life experiences and learning. Whether or not you are aware of them, you have your own unique set.

There is a simple way to determine what your core values are. Though simple, the exercise may take hours (or days) to zero in on your true core values. So give yourself enough time to complete this exercise. It could change your life.

With a little research, I found more than four hundred words describing values. Here's a partial list:

| | | |
|---|---|---|
| Abundance | Equality | Loyalty |
| Acceptance | Excellence | Obedience |
| Accomplishment | Fairness | Openness |
| Adaptability | Faith | Patriotism |
| Adventure | Fidelity | Perfection |
| Ambition | Fitness | Professionalism |
| Accuracy | Focus | Relationships |
| Achievement | Freedom | Reliability |
| Adventure | Fun | Reputation |
| Assertiveness | Generosity | Restraint |
| Balance | Goodness | Reverence |
| Belonging | Growth | Security |
| Challenge | Harmony | Simplicity |
| Commitment | Honesty | Strength |
| Community | Humility | Structure |
| Compassion | Holiness | Teamwork |
| Competitiveness | Independence | Toughness |
| Control | Individuality | Transparency |
| Cooperation | Integrity | Trust |
| Creativity | Joy | Unity |
| Dedication | Justice | Vitality |
| Discipline | Leadership | Warmth |
| Diversity | Love | Zeal |

1. Review the list of values and check the ones that fit you. Be very careful to not romanticize or fall in love with a value that you would like to espouse, but never will. For example: You wish you could be a real team player, but you know you never will be. If that's the case, don't pick that particular value.

2. Think about your proudest and happiest moments. What values were represented in those moments?

3. Now, think of the most negative, angry, and frustrating moments of your life. Chances are you were angry and upset about a value being violated. Underline those.

4. Look at all the values you checked and underlined.

5. Winnow your list to 10 values you consider to be most important to you. Remember, these are *your* values.

6. From your list of 10 values, circle the 5 that are most important to you. In your own words write a brief definition of each.

7. Rank those five in order of importance. The top three are likely your core values.

Review your list every day for the next week or so. You might realize that you made a few choices that don't feel exactly right. That's okay. Revise your list until you are satisfied with it. Then reflect on how well your life matches up with your values.

## ON THE JOB

According to a 2014 Pew Research Center study, about 10% of the U.S. workforce is self-employed.

That means 90% of us are working for, or looking for work with an employer of some sort.

The other 10% must answer to their customers and clients.

Our bosses, whether they are our employers or our clients, get to dictate what we do and when we do it, controlling our lives for 40-50 hours per week, or more.

When our time and actions are controlled by others, *their* values can become *our* values, creating a values chasm.

• • •

Amy had identified her top values as integrity, faith, and relationships. Initially, Amy felt that her job aligned well with her values. She could see a clear connection between her work and patients receiving quality care at reasonable costs. She cultivated significant relationships with her clients and did all she could to ensure that they received the best service possible.

Hers was a high-paying job in the healthcare industry. She regularly earned cash bonuses and was awarded stock options. Her job also required frequent travels, which she enjoyed,.

Her boss fought to seek and maintain parity in pay between Amy and her male counterparts. All was good.

But then a change in company leadership shifted the business model. Shareholder gain and stock value became the company's top priorities. Gone was the goal to balance profit with employee and customer satisfaction. The staff was presented with ever increasing sales goals while bonus potential and personal rewards decreased.

Amy's habit of going above and beyond on behalf of her customers was suddenly frowned upon—unless, of course, it meant more billing revenue. The changing culture created a pressure cooker atmosphere where long hours were the norm and customer satisfaction took a back seat to extracting every dollar possible from clients.

Amy was experiencing a shift in the balance of her intrinsic and extrinsic motivations. Her intrinsic motivation—doing things that she really liked and had a passion for doing—was being replaced by extrinsic motivation, which meant she was doing things only because they resulted in rewards.

As time went on, her passionate engagement dwindled. Soon, it became harder for her to achieve the same rewards as she had before. If she failed to reach her maximum sales goal she risked being fired. Even though Amy's immediate boss recognized what was happening, he was powerless in changing the overall culture of the organization.

Amy was unhappy. Unable to nurture her client relationships as she had before, she had lost faith in a company that put profits ahead of people.

Though Amy considered moving on to a new job, she faced a conundrum. She wasn't happy, but she was still highly compensated. Her salary afforded her a comfortable lifestyle which she didn't want to give up.

She realized that her job no longer was in sync with her values, but she was hostage to her salary, stock options, and bonuses.

Fortunately, though it didn't feel so fortunate at the time, the company laid off a number of high-paid individuals, including Amy.

She used her newfound freedom to locate a position with a company whose values more closely matched hers.

• • •

A number of years ago, on a business trip to St. Augustine, Florida, several of my colleagues and I went out to dinner at a local restaurant.

Our server, who was perhaps in his mid-twenties, was exceptionally engaging. At some point during our dinner, I asked the waiter what his "deal" was. I asked, "Are you a student?" thinking he was studying toward my idea of something bigger and better.

His response surprised me.

"No, I'm a server," he said. "This is what I choose to do for a living. The job is portable. I can work almost anywhere. I work from about 4:00 p.m. until 10:00 p.m., five or six nights a week. The rest of the time is mine do as I please. I surf. I read books. I ride a bike. I take naps. Waiting tables provides enough money for me to live the life I choose to live."

This young man knew his values. Furthermore, he was living them.

He was more content than any one of us at the table. He knew his job was simply a means to an end.

For the rest of the night, my tablemates and I tried to count the endless hours we spent in hotels, on airplanes, and away from home while seeking something we could not fully describe.

In the end, we all agreed—our waiter was living his dream. He knew what was important in his life, and he pursued it wholeheartedly.

Given his values, this young man was wildly successful. He had no need to "set **the** world on fire."

His wanted to set **his** world on fire.

Since his needs were met, he was content and happy.


## Ongoing Process

The encounter with the St. Augustine waiter occurred nearly 20 years ago and it set me on a course that would change my life. The waiter is one of my heroes who proved that when our lives match our values, we are fulfilled and energized. Life is good. Our conversation made me think about my values and how they aligned with fulfilling my needs and desires.

Suddenly, I was re-evaluating my life. In terms of Maslow's needs, I was severely out of balance. I was sharply focused on esteem and self-actualization. My physical and safety needs were more than met. However, my relationship and spiritual needs were lacking and nearly devoid.

Since the waiter awoke my interest in values, I realized that needs and values are not static, and therefore, I began taking stock of mine on a regular basis

Knowing that our values change over time, repeating the value finder exercise every six months or so helps us keep tabs on our values. As you do so, check your life's alignment with your current situation. Ask yourself the following questions:

- What are my values and needs?
- Are they aligned with my life?
- How are my needs/values reflected in my life goals?
- What am I doing to satisfy my needs/values?
- Do my job, hobbies, and activities align with my needs/values?
- How might I realign my needs/values?
- Is there an incremental way to satisfy any misalignment?

Answers to these questions should lead you to furthering the goals you've set for yourself.

*I can do things you cannot,*
*you can do things I cannot,*
*together we can do great things.*

—Mother Teresa

# Everyone is Smarter 6

THE TITLE OF THIS CHAPTER is a reminder that there is a wealth of knowledge that can be gleaned from others. Millions of people know things we do not know. Some know how to solve a quadratic equation. Others know how to play polo or fly an airplane. I know plenty of people who are smarter than me when it comes to many things. For example, approximately 341 million people speak English as their first language, while more than twice that number, roughly 874 million, speak Mandarin Chinese. Right there, more than three quarters of a BILLION people are smarter than me. How about you?

Living a life well lived is not about standing in judgment of others' brainpower. It is about leveraging your interactions with others to your benefit and perhaps theirs too.

Dr. Laurie Ferguson, Ph.D., Vice president of Education for Creaky Joints, an online Patient Community says, "You shouldn't go it alone." Our brains aren't built for us to go it alone. She says when accompanied by someone else, even a trusted stranger, the patient feels less anxious. With another by his side, Ferguson reports, the patient feels more capable and he may even experience less pain.

What does all of this have to do with you and living the life of your dreams? Everything! By not going it alone, you may feel more capable and experience less trauma and stress. Who doesn't want that?

It's not just about the people, it's about the various life lessons that come to you through books, travel, personal interactions, relationships, and more. As we experience all of these things, we distill this amalgamation of life into our own unique perspectives and mindsets.

In the appendix, you will find a list of books which influenced my life and helped cement the ideas brought forth in this book. Some of the books (in my opinion) contain a treasure trove of information, and others have but a snippet of information that was influential.

I learned about "Juicing the Jam" from *Top Performer: A Proven Way to Dramatically Boost Your Sales and Yourself* by Stephen C. Lundin. Lundin points out that regardless what we do for a living, we are all in sales; we must sell our value to our bosses, clients, or customers.

From time to time in our sales processes things will go wrong. That is when Lundin advises thinking like a street performer who drops the chain saw he is juggling. It wasn't meant to happen, but the performer must now "Juice the Jam" to recover from the mistake. How does he do that? Usually, the street performer recovers by making light of the situation and feigning it as a planned event to make his audience laugh.

Once, at a national conference in front of a room with more than a hundred people, the session moderator showed the first slide of his presentation. Facing his audience, he heard mild laughter and snickers.

He turned around and looked at the title slide. It said, "Pubic Risk Management," as opposed to "*Public* Risk Management." Without missing a beat, he said, "What? I ran the spell checker. It's spelled right. It's just the wrong word and you should manage *that* too, but that's not what we're here to talk about today." He "Juiced the Jam" and carried on.

Not all of us are street performers and we can't continually make light of the "screw ups" that happen along the way. Sometimes we get by with making an excuse, but excuses are short-lived and eventually you will be found out. We're best off owning up to mistakes and making things right: look at what happened, find its cause, and keep it from happening again.

Suppose you have been reading about the temples of Angkor Wat and you make a decision that you want to visit. If you live in the United States, the temples are located nearly half-way around the world. Would you rather go alone, or with someone else?

Most of us would likely choose to travel with someone as opposed to going it alone. Having a travel companion not only provides someone with whom to immediately share experiences, but also gives us someone to lean on and help navigate the challenges of international travel.

Even without a travel companion to help you through the inevitable travails of travel, my advice is to go for it anyway. There will be many opportunities for you to learn from and lean on strangers along the way.

I once took a two-week trip around-the-world, myself—no traveling companion. The first four days were for business, the rest of the trip for pleasure.

In the beginning of the trip, I felt alone, but soon realized my trip was supported by a wide range of people smarter than me. About 12 hours into my flight from Los Angeles to Sydney, Australia, the Captain came on with the following announcement.

*Ladies and gentlemen, I have some good news and some bad news. The bad news is that we have been fighting a strong headwind throughout this flight. That has caused us to use more fuel than normal and we won't have enough fuel to make it to Sydney. The good news is: We can stop in Brisbane to get fuel.*

As our plane flew on, I got to thinking about my trip. For me, it seemed like a pretty big adventure and it was, but then I thought about the huge network of smart people who made my trip possible.

Air travel has come a long way since the Wright brothers first lifted off, going 120-200 feet at 6.8 mph. Behind today's modern air transportation is a huge network of people smarter than many of us. There are aeronautical engineers who design and innovate aircraft construction. Computer scientists assist in the design and help automate flight systems. Others design radio communications and global positioning systems. The ticket and gate agents tell us where to go and when to be there. The pilot has his co-pilot. A large network of air traffic controllers work diligently to keep aircraft separate and safe.

I soon realized that I was anything but alone flying some 6 and half miles above the ocean at 550 mph.

As I pondered the synergy of all who made this possible, the Captain interrupted with another announcement.

*Ladies and gentlemen, I have some more good news and some more bad news. The bad news is that we did the calculations and figured out that stopping in Brisbane for fuel and going on to Sydney will have us landing in Sydney at 11:01 p.m.*

*For those of you who don't know, the Sydney airport is located very close to the city and has a strict curfew for landings and take-offs after 11:00 p.m. We have requested a variance and it has been denied. The good news is that Qantas Airlines will transport you by motor coach and put you up in a hotel tonight in Brisbane.*

As I thought, *Now what?* the captain came back.

*I'm also sorry to say that I have more good news and bad news. The good news is that we will continue on to Sydney tomorrow morning. The bad news is we leave for Sydney at 7:00 in the morning.*

The system had kicked in and a bunch of people smarter than me had figured out the logistics to find hotel rooms, get us there, and return us to the airport in the early morning hours. That folks, is synergy in action!

The next morning, at the airport, there was a fairly long line at check-in. I struck up a conversation with people standing near me in the queue.

The woman behind me in line was from Ohio and must have been one of the most important people in the world because she was very upset that we'd had to stop in Brisbane for only a few hours' sleep. Her first day in Sydney, she said, was going to be ruined. The overnight delay was absolutely the worst thing ever. *Holy crap lady!* I thought, *Get a grip.*

The man ahead of me was Australian, born and raised in Sydney, and was returning home after business in Los Angeles. His wife had warned him to not cut his travel plans too closely because they were leaving that morning on a trip to celebrate her 50th birthday.

Because of our flight delay the night before, he was going to miss their departure and disappoint his wife. This apparently wasn't the first time something like this happened. However, he never failed to bring her something special from his travels and he said she had learned to take his frequent absences and un-avoidable delays in stride. He was confident that she would understand and all would be well.

He told me that Brisbane was a great city to visit and suggested that if ever I returned to his fine country, I should give Brisbane a whirl.

I said how I was happy to get to see an extra city and to be put up in a great hotel. Plus, I found XXXX Gold Lager in my mini-bar—one of the best beers of the trip. After my favorable comments, the woman from Ohio said, "What are you, a preacher?" I said, "No Ma'am, I'm just an optimist."

When I boarded the plane, I found myself sitting next to a young woman about 18 years old. She, too, was traveling alone. During our flight to Sydney, she said she was going there because her sponsor was opening a new retail store.

When I asked about her "sponsor," she told me about her adventures as a professional surfer. She was about half my age and had already been around the world a number of times. (Her favorite surfing spot was off the coast of South Africa.) We talked about our mutual zest for life and as we parted, I said, "Go get 'em!" She winked and gave me that famous surfer "Shaka" hand signal which means "Hang loose."

Though this entire trip was filled with interesting interactions, this one was a highlight. That young woman was clearly living a bold life. Hearing about her adventures emboldened me for the rest of my trip, and frankly, my life. She confirmed that we can all achieve great things if we just pursue them. If someone less than half my age could be that adventurous, so could I!

A lot was gained on this trip, all due to the fact that everyone around me knew things that I didn't. Because of our pilot's training and experience, and due to the network of people on the ground supporting him, our plane didn't run out of fuel and fall into the Pacific Ocean. The Australian businessman showed me the importance of taking care of personal relationships. The woman from Ohio, on the other hand, because she viewed the whole experience as a great inconvenience to her, allowed her trip to be ruined, and modeled the importance of keeping things in perspective.

## PERSONAL INFLUENCERS

Even when you might think you are alone, you rarely are completely alone. There are almost always others around who know exactly what you need to know.

We all have different bodies of knowledge and we can leverage others' wisdom and knowledge as we pursue our dreams. Being conscious of another's expertise and personal take on life provides invaluable lessons—both positive and negative. The following are some of the relationships that influenced my life. They appear in no particular order, but my parents are first.

## MY FOLKS

Except for a doctor and a few nurses, my parents were the first people I ever met the day I was born at what was then Deaconess Hospital on Wisconsin Avenue in downtown Milwaukee.

I loved my parents and they taught me many life lessons. Reflecting back on their lives, I'm pretty sure they never fully achieved the life of their dreams, but they had a good life.

They had three very strong and distinct social groups— family, church, and work. Through those three groups, I learned a lot about living a great life.

It is difficult to quantify the numerous lessons I learned from their social interactions with people at church, work, and amongst family members. Perhaps the biggest lesson was to be generous. They modeled generosity with their time and money for the good of the community and their friends. Mom and Dad were always planning the next party, the next menu, the next opportunity to laugh and have a good time.

Today, I am carrying on the tradition.

## UNCLE FRANK

Frank Piasecki was my godfather and a character, or to use his term for a person with a peculiar characteristic, "a canary."

Frank was of a slender build, slightly germophobic, fastidious, with his hair always neatly groomed, thanks to the help of Brylcreem. His skin had a bronze tone from all of the time he spent outdoors fishing.

Frank was also opinionated with a quick temper that subsided as quickly as it came on.

He was a relentless teaser. He might make fun of your name, your clothing, or your haircut. He tickled us kids, took off our shoes, turned us upside down, and pinched our cheeks until we cried for mercy. As soon as we regained our balance, we ran right back for more.

For a time, Uncle Frank lived next door to Reggie Lisowski, a professional wrestler known as "The Crusher." His workout was running with a full keg of beer on his shoulder. The workout was done when the keg was empty.

One Labor Day, our extended family had a cookout at

Frank's house. The party began around four o'clock in the afternoon. As usual, the party sprawled from the house, to the two-car garage, and onto the driveway. There might have been as many as 25 people there at peak.

As the party was winding down, around eight p.m, The Crusher came over and complained about the music (polkas playing on the record player).

My Uncle Frank stood up to him and said, "We'll be done when we're done."

The Crusher responded by picking up the record player and throwing it across the garage. "There will be no more music," he said.

Despite the wrestler's size and muscled advantage over Frank, Frank confronted him toe to toe. Neither backed down and the police were called. Before they arrived Frank got punched in the face and ended up with a doozy of a shiner.

Frank was a foreman at a local foundry. I worked there during the summers while I was in college. I never worked for him directly and was careful to not mention our relationship.

I soon learned that Frank's employees either loved him or severely disliked him. If you were a hard worker, showed up on time, and rarely missed work, Frank would do anything for you. If you fell on the other end of the spectrum, forget it. (People in that camp wrote "Frank Sucks" on a concrete wall.)

Frank never knew a stranger. He could talk with anyone.

He attended all the social events (weddings, birthdays and funerals) hosted by his best workers and was often the only Caucasian at the event.

He was an interesting dichotomy. He seemingly knew few boundaries, yet he kept to the familiar. Frank often travelled to the same places for vacation and ate in only familiar restaurants. Every Saturday night was "steak night."

Though not particularly bold himself, Frank always encouraged others to be bold and to take on new adventures. Perhaps he lived vicariously.

I'm glad I took his advice. I'm proud to say I've marched to the beat of my own drummer, I've learned to never back down; and I've never met a stranger.

## Miss Hahn

Picture a golden-haired, slender, and younger version of Aunt Bea from *The Andy Griffith Show*—that would be Miss Eunice Hahn, my high school guidance counselor.

I met Miss Hahn after a pretty rough junior high experience. Don't get me wrong, I wasn't bad, I just wasn't very good. At that point, I wasn't interested at all in school.

Miss Hahn "got me." Somehow, she could relate to me on a personal level at a time when I was awkward and unsure of myself. Rather than telling me what I should be doing, she asked what mattered to me.

Despite her expert guidance, I never excelled in high school. Her guidance helped me stay on track and kept me from spiraling out of control. With her help, I maintained the minimum and made it to graduation.

Her guidance was like a time-released pill. The full effect wasn't felt until after I'd left high school. After a detour, I applied for college. Thanks to Miss Hahn's persistence and guidance, my records were good enough to be accepted. As a college student, so much of what she'd told me became relevant and I was able to hold my own.

I checked in with her from time to time to let her know that I was finally following her advice. Twenty years after high school, I wrote her a letter thanking her for the profound influence she'd had on me. May she rest in peace knowing, as they say in the South—"She done good!"

## GUY

It's not always the best characters who become our influencers. Bad examples can teach some mighty fine lessons, too. I once worked for a man who lived a miserable existence. Without going into the details of his life, let's suffice it to say, he was an unhappy man and a bad boss. Let's call this guy "Guy."

Guy was my boss in what could have been an idyllic situation. Our office, in a quaint southern California city, was two blocks from the Pacific Ocean. I was well compensated at this job.

Office hours were eight to five. And by golly, you better be on time. Guy's office was next to the back door where most employees entered the building. At about 7:55 each morning, Guy would position himself at his office door and greet everyone. Then, he would hang out for about 30 minutes to greet late comers. If you were five minutes late, Guy might say, "Glad you could join us." If you were 15-20 minutes late, he'd tell you, "Good afternoon."

Lunchtime was noon until one—no exceptions. At exactly twelve noon, Guy and the occupants of the three offices immediately adjacent to his would step from their offices, look at each other, nod, close their doors, and head to lunch. This was done with near military precision.

I kept a beach chair in my office and a small group of us often ate lunch at the beach, watching the surfers, roller skaters, bikers, and volleyball players. But woe unto us if we weren't back at our desks at one sharp.

Even if you were stuck on the phone with a client, or in a meeting that lasted past noon, your lunch hour ended at one. After lunch, Guy repeated his morning drill. Get caught in Southern California traffic while at lunch and arrive back late, Guy would be there to greet you. Grown men and women ran back to the office to avoid the wrath of Guy.

Do you know what happened at five? Correct, everyone vanished. No one put in any extra effort for that boss.

Our company budgets were done by "line item," meaning there were specific lines for various types of expenses. One of my line items was a small budget for one professional magazine subscription. The subscription was paid in the first month of our fiscal year and usually used up 98% of the money budgeted for that line. When the first month's financials came out, Guy was in my office saying, "What are you going to do for the rest of the year?" Though I explained, it was the one expense for that line for the entire year, he was in my office each month with the same question.

When our payroll clerk turned 50, the maintenance department cut a large five and a zero out of pieces of plywood, painted them red, and put them in front of her desk. As Guy and I walked by her desk, he whispered to me under his breath, "That fiftieth birthday is costing us a fortune."

I could go on for several more pages about Guy's peculiarities, but you get the picture. It didn't take long to get fed up with Guy's antics. Micromanagement was not for me.

As my career progressed and I became the boss, I've used the lessons Guy taught me to remind me to be more flexible and compassionate.

## AL

Remember "Mr. Clean," the signature figure of Proctor and Gamble's all-purpose cleaner? That tall, muscular, calm and self-assured man, minus the earring, looks like my former boss Al Hyman.

To call Al a boss is misleading. He never really bossed me. When my travel expenses were getting a bit high, all he said was, "You might want to watch those, because you are in the lead of a category that you don't want to lead."

Al always has a smile and a story. His career ranged from being a life guard on the Chicago beaches to being an insurance expert who appeared on *Good Morning America*. Al was the guru, the Dalai Lama, of our industry. His calm demeanor, vast knowledge, and sense of self made him the "go-to" resource. And his advice was sought literally around the world.

When I first went to work for Al, I was a little apprehensive. I said, "I'm not sure I know what I'm supposed to do." He said, "When the phone rings, you'll know what to do." He was correct. When the phone started ringing, I knew what to do and was able to do it because my boss trusted me to do a good job and at the same time, he knew I would ask him questions when I needed guidance.

During our time working together, we traveled extensively and with that we developed a code. After travelling most of a week, he and I might say to one another, "I'm going to lay low today." That meant, "don't bother me, I'm heading to the golf course." He was the kind of boss who recognized the importance of down time and recharging.

As a leader, teacher, and friend, he taught me about gentleness, self-deprecation, and patience. He is humble and secure in who he is. He always found a way to get what he was looking for with a smile, soft words, and a couple of bucks. He underscored my desire to be generous and kind.

• • •

Potential influencers surround us every day. Observe the child who makes a toy of the simplest of objects. Listen to the wise advice from the woman sitting next to you on the park bench. Follow someone else's lead and choose to emulate a positive characteristic from a person you observe in the wild!

## CREATING SYNERGY

When we recognize that others can help us "tackle" most any venture, we find out that it isn't so lonely going after even the most daunting of tasks. Through others' examples we learn the things we don't already know, and our endeavors are enhanced through this synergy.

When the sum of the parts equals more than the individual pieces this is the definition of synergy.

For a few years, I was an adjunct professor in Insurance and Risk Management at the University of North Carolina at Charlotte. It was one of the most rewarding experiences of my lifetime and was enhanced by the synergy found between me and another professor. He was the academic who literally wrote the book on the subject; I was the practitioner who applied the theories.

In preparation, I studied the textbooks. In them, I discovered a significant difference between theory and reality.

In the beginning, I found myself to be rusty on some of the theories. Likewise, I found my associate had never applied the theories in real life. His theories were not wrong, but he was unaware that practical application of those theories involved combining them with other theories. Sometimes it was necessary to take shortcuts, and sometimes we had to ignore theory all together.

Neither one of us was wrong, but without each other we weren't exactly correct either. It took the combination of our knowledge to present the whole picture.

Our synergy paid off. We instructors learned from each other while teaching our students both the theory and the reality. Former students who are now well entrenched in the industry have stayed in touch and affirm that our combined approach gave them a better understanding of the theories and their practical application.

## MASTERMIND

In 1937, Napoleon Hill introduced the concept of the "master mind alliance" in his book, *Think and Grow Rich*. Hill hypoth-

*It's not what you know,*
*it's who you know.*

—Napoleon Hill

esized that two heads were better than one and when collaboration between two or more minds occurred, it resulted in a "master mind." Hill said, "No two minds ever come together without, thereby, creating a third, invisible, intangible force which may be likened to a third mind."

Hill wrote about Andrew Carnegie's staff of about 50 individuals whose sole purpose was to help him manufacture and market steel. Carnegie's mastermind group helped him make a fortune and forge an everlasting legacy.

Among Carnegie's mastermind group were the likes of Charles M. Schwab who rose from a laborer position in his early working life to become a manager for Andrew Carnegie's steel business. Schwab later aligned himself with J.P. Morgan and together they combined multiple steel companies (including Carnegie's) to form U. S. Steel. They were further aligned with other famous men like the Vanderbilts and Rockefellers.

Need I say more about the value of a mastermind alliance?

Your mastermind group does not have to be a formalized group. It can be a wide collection of individuals whose brains you pick for information. Through interactions with them you can formulate, develop, and improve your own thoughts and ideas. With the exception of my editor/publisher and my awesome wife, few in my mastermind group even know they are serving in this role for my book.

Recently, my wife and I had a completely random encounter with a waitress at one of our favorite restaurants. While talking about wine with the waitress, we told her we splurged a bit because we were celebrating my having finished the first draft of this book. The waitress then revealed that she was a medical doctor by training and had moved to our area to be near her ailing mother. She went on to tell us about one of her friends who had written a book and used a unique marketing strategy to move it to a best seller list. You never know where your masterminds lay. (We'll see how the strategy works for this book.)

Mastermind input need not always be positive. A former employee once told me, "Dan, your problem is that you want everyone to like you." I think she wanted me to take on a meaner demeanor. I don't recall responding to her comment, but thought to myself, "Having everyone 'like' me seems to be a pretty good goal." So I did the exact opposite of her advice and worked to treat everyone fairly and with decency. That doesn't mean I turned into a milquetoast. I held to my principles, but became a gentler soul.

Mastermind advice can come when you least expect it. After an unbelievable three-day stay in Rome I was heading to the airport to go to London for a few nights. The taxi driver was Italian, but had lived in a number of places in Europe and for several years in Hawaii.

During my ride, the driver quizzed me about my stay, what I did, and places I visited. I made a flippant comment about him making sure I spent enough money while I was there to keep the economy going. He remained cordial, but said, "You Americans, your focus is in the wrong place. It's not about the money, it's about enjoying the moments and experiences to be had in a place so rich in sights and experiences."

My driver was right; my focus was off. I had had a marvelous time over the previous three days, but had failed to appreciate being in the moment. In just a few seconds, this taxi driver imparted not only some solid travel advice, but some outstanding life advice. We should all savor every moment of our short lives.

# Life's Too Short 7

HOUGH THIS CHAPTER is about time, it is about so much more. It's about understanding time so you can use it to your maximum benefit and live the life of your dreams. It means not wasting time on the inconsequential. It's about living your life deliberately and exploring the various forks in the road. Above all, it is about life being too short to continue doing things you would rather not be doing.

How short is life? In 2015, according to the United States Center for Disease Control, an American's average life expectancy was 78.6 years. To put that in perspective, consider that the earth is estimated to be 4.6 billion years old—about 59 million times our lifespan. The extinction of dinosaurs occurred about 66 million years ago—almost 840,000 such lifespans.

Given that, our lives are but a brief blip—way too short to not make the most of it.

Time is also relative, not in the Albert Einstein Theory of Relativity sense (I don't think), but relative to how we experience life as we mature. Depending on your perspective, 78.6 years may seem like a long time. As a child, you may have calculated the year in which you would turn a certain age and when you did, the calculated date might have seemed to be eons into the future. Then, before you knew it, you are at that age and feel like you just did the calculation yesterday.

In a *Scientific American*, article "Why Does Time Seem to Speed Up with Age?" James M. Broadway cites what psychologist Claudia Hammond calls the holiday paradox. When you are younger, you encounter many new experiences and learn new skills. During those new experiences, your brain records most of the specific details of the encounter. Upon recollection, because there is more detail to recall, it only seems like it lasted longer. As we age and repeat experiences, they aren't recorded in our brains with nearly the same amount of detail. Without the details, there is less to remember and thus seems to have occurred in significantly less time.

Think about the first time you went to a favorite restaurant. You may recall the sights, sounds, smells, tastes, what you wore, and the company you kept. As you worked your way through the experience, you recorded every savory bite while you en-

coupled with its furtive timing, you would serve yourself well to stop and think about your precious life at this given moment.

Few would argue that there is anything more important than maintaining connections to those who are close to you. With that said, you owe it to yourself and them to communicate their worth. Before you go any further, consider these questions and act on them as soon as possible:

- Who do you love? Do they know?

  *If yes, tell 'em again. If no, pick up the phone, seek them out, and tell them!*

- Are you at peace with your parents, siblings, or extended family?

  *If so, that's awesome—could you do more to strengthen those relationships? If you are not at peace, reach out and at least tell them you wish things were different. Not all family feuds can be settled in a short time, but signaling peace covers you if you were to check-out unexpectedly.*

- Is there someone from your past you've been putting off contacting?

  *Seek them out. Say hello. Let them know you were thinking of them.*

- Is there someone you need to forgive?

  *If so, forgive them. If possible, forgive them person to per-*

*son. If that is not possible because they are completely gone from your life, or perhaps dead, forgive them in your mind. The universe will connect you.*

- If you are a spiritual person, are you at peace with your God? *If so, great. If not, have a talk with Him or Her.*

Taking those actions may help you avoid what happened to me. Charlie was a larger than life figure. He was tall and steady with graying hair, a deep husky voice, and a prominent nose. He was probably old enough to be my father and perhaps even my grandfather. He had a reputation of being brusque and difficult. When assigned to work with Charlie, I wondered what I had done to deserve this punishment.

My first encounter with him occurred on the shop floor. He didn't say a word after I told him I was assigned to him. He just shook his right hand as if he were shaking water from it and walked away.

*Holy crap*, I thought.

Over time, we found a way to work together and became friends. We were both early birds and often met in his office first thing in the morning. One such morning, I showed up at his office, found it dark with the door closed and locked. It was unlike Charlie to be late. After some time, his assistant arrived with a grim look on her face. Charlie had died knotting his tie before he came to work.

This wasn't my first experience with someone close to me dying. However, Charlie's death affected me like no other. It haunted me for months when almost every idle moment was filled with thoughts of him. Charlie and I had left things unsaid. Charlie taught me how to look at the big picture, cut through the superfluous, and get on with the job at hand. I think our working together somehow softened his once harder outside shell.

Maybe Charlie's passing would have been the same had we shared more of our feelings, but his sudden departure from this earth will always leave me wondering. All I can say is, rest in peace, Charlie. You were a good man.

Making things right with others is not always easy, but doing so frees your mind. Once you've squared yourself with others, you can deliberately move on with living the life that makes you you.

## Don't Waste Time on the Unimportant

It is up to each of us to determine what is important, and what can wait until later.

We recognize that the needs for food, safety, and shelter are fundamental. To satisfy those needs, most of us have to work at least 40 hours a week. For 95% of the American workforce, that means commuting to the workplace. (5% of us work from

*Things which matter most must never be at the mercy of things which matter least.*

—Goethe

home.)

In 2015, Americans endured/enjoyed an average commute of just under 30 minutes each way; about 20% of them spent 60 minutes each way. Some spent even more time.

An average commuter then, spends about five hours per week commuting. Assuming 2 weeks of vacation, 250 hours per year are spent by the average person just getting to and from work. Based on an eight-hour workday, it's as if we are spending 31.25 days in the car and it is unpaid at that! On a 24-hour per day basis, you're spending more than 10 full days commuting.

Wouldn't you agree that you should take advantage of the time? Look around next time you are driving in to work. You will probably see people driving with dazed looks on their faces. You may see them having a heated telephone conversation, or worse, see them texting, or checking Facebook. Too many of us are wasting our commute on the inconsequential.

On public transit, you might see much of the same, though you will see more people sleeping, reading, or immersed in their own inner sanctum behind their ear buds. If it weren't for the fact that our commute is the only way to get to work, I'm pretty sure we all would pass up the commute. When have you ever heard anyone say, "I'm off today, but am going drive to the office and back anyway?"

The commute then is essential, but what many of us do with that time is worthless. You drive to and from work barely aware of how you got to where you were going. You get ticked off when some idiot pulls in front of you and then go into a rage when you don't make it through the traffic light that he did.

Calm down, folks.

The commute does not have to be inconsequential, it can be a vital part of moving your life to the next level. If you drive by yourself, it can be a good time to do some deep thinking about the next steps of your life. Consider getting a handheld voice recorder to make notes of important actions or steps, but be careful to remain attentive to traffic and conditions so as not to become distracted and involved in a crash.

The commute can also be an opportunity to learn something new—you can listen to an audiobook or a podcast. Listen to something that you had hoped to read some day, or listen to something that you might never do otherwise. I listened to *Don Quixote* and the *Fifty Shades of Grey* books during my commute, things I would have never have sat down and read otherwise.

Speaking of *Fifty Shades of Grey*, author, E. L. James says her first book was written largely with the help of notes she made to herself on a BlackBerry while commuting to and from work. She would upload the notes to her computer and continue writing when she got home. Over the course of two years, she completed the first book. As a result, she is now living the life of her dreams.

Your life as a commuter is only one place where you might

be sacrificing valuable time to focus on the unimportant. Perhaps it's time for you to take an inventory of your daily activities to see where you are really spending your precious time.

There is no need to do an extensive minute by minute inventory. For the next several days, don't modify what you usually do, but keep track (see the chart in the appendices) of how you spend your time on the following:

- Sleeping
- Personal grooming
- Commuting
- Working
- Watching television
- Other screen time (including time spent at work)
- Meal preparation
- Eating
- Exercising
- Hobbies
- Reading/Self-Improvement
- Household chores
- Child care
- Other

Where are you spending your time? Is it all necessary? Could a different haircut or make-up routine cut your primping time? Are you watching mindless television? Can you eliminate unproductive and unimportant time wasters in preference of new pursuits that will move you closer to where you would like to go?

All of us have 24 hours each a day. It is up to us to use them wisely.

## GET HAPPY AND BE HAPPY

Scientists at the University of North Carolina conducted a 30-year study with 30,000 participants and concluded that happier people live longer. They found the risk of death to be 6% higher for those who reported being pretty happy as opposed to very happy. In comparing unhappy to very happy, there was a 14% difference in death rates.

What does it mean to be happy? The Merriam-Webster dictionary offers a number of definitions. My two favorites are, "favored by luck or fortune" and "notably fitting, effective, or well adapted." The latter definition helps to create the former. To accomplish both takes conscious effort.

A quick search revealed hundreds of books on happiness. With the wide array of books on the subject, I'm led to believe we might be experiencing a happiness crisis.

Digging into the available writings on happiness I found that there are anywhere between 2 and 31 types of happiness. I zeroed in on two experts, one academic and one from the world of business, and it is surprising how closely their theories match.

Dr. Paul T. Wong, Professor Emeritus of Trent University in Peterborough, Ontario Canada, described four types of happiness:

- HEDONIC: The pleasant moments such as "eat, drink and be merry"
- PRUDENTIAL: The "flow" or enjoyment of doing what one does best
- EUDAEMONIC: A sense of fulfillment or flourishing from the pursuit of meaning and virtue
- CHARONIC: The feeling of being blessed or favored by God

Tony Hsieh, founder and CEO of Zappo's, listed the 3 P's of happiness:

- PLEASURE
- PASSION
- HIGHER PURPOSE

Both models are similar in that the most basic level of happiness is what the academics call hedonic pleasure. Hsieh describes this level of happiness as the pleasure a rock star experiences when playing to a sold-out audience. The pleasure might be somewhat tactile and fleeting. Once the concert is over, the pleasure fades.

In seeking happiness, be careful. Deriving pleasure at that hedonic level can be habit forming. Losing control of that habit can lead to addiction. Over time, we build a tolerance for the pleasurable activity and we need more and more of the habit to create our fleeting pleasure and happiness. We can become addicted to most anything—drugs, alcohol, video games, social media, sex. Once addicted, it may lead to feelings of despair when we no longer experience the same euphoria from our chosen habit. Constantly chasing hedonic pleasures can leave us feeling empty and may be a cause of increased depression, unhappiness, and in extreme cases even suicide.

This is not to say all habits are bad. Maintaining a habit of going to work, providing for family, obeying laws, etc. contribute to our overall well-being. When pursuing hedonic pleasure enters an endless loop, we become stuck seeking bigger and shinier experiences to replace the ones that no longer satisfy us. This is where moving to the next level of happiness is key.

Wong's middle two levels coincide with Hsieh's second level: passion. In this stage, happiness is brought about by engaging in what one really loves to do while pursuing meaning and virtue. Happiness then, is not a destination; rather, it is a practice! This might be where casual golfers become serious golfers. They begin to achieve a level of mastery that makes them want to dive deeper into the game.

At the passion level, it isn't all fun and happiness. Work mixes with pleasure. This is where our golfer crosses over from merely playing the game, to studying the game, practicing, taking lessons, and learning what it takes to move to the next level. Passion, or the eudaemonic stage, is nowhere as fleeting as the hedonic stage, but it may not last forever.

Dean's love for the game began as a social event to share some laughs, drink a few beers, and have fun with some friends. Over time, he became an avid golfer. Dean built a house on the golf course and joined the golf club, and played three or four times a week. Golf was his passion and he was having fun.

One day, playing with some friends, they were on the 12th hole. It had been rainy and the golf carts were required to stay on the cart path. Dean's tee shot was pretty good. He drove the cart up the path, even with his ball in the fairway. Dean selected the club for his second shot, walked out to the ball, addressed it, and hit it. The shot wasn't bad, nor was it particularly good.

Dean was pleased with his 12 handicap, but he knew his game wasn't going to get much better without adding a significant amount of time and work.

Walking back to the cart, Dean suddenly thought, *I'm just not having fun at this anymore.* He finished the round and pretty much quit playing. He had burned out his passion. It was time to move on to something else.

Another case in point is Dave Del Dotto. After amassing a fortune through various entrepreneurial ventures, he moved his family to Hawaii and planned to live out his life in leisure.

Pretty soon, Del Dotto said wanting for nothing left him

empty. There is, he said, only so much 1947 Bordeaux that one can drink. Nonetheless, he took his family to vacation in the California wine country. At one vineyard, his family waited in the car for him, thinking he was tasting yet another wine.

Instead, he was negotiating to purchase the winery. Today, instead of lazing on some beach in Hawaii, he and his family are pursuing a new passion in Napa Valley.

The ultimate attainment of happiness is the charonic, or higher purpose stage. Bill Gates is likely a good example of someone in this stage. Gates spent many years in the first two stages of happiness as he passionately pursued building Microsoft into the giant that it is today. Now, he is able to reach a higher purpose in life by using his vast wealth to solve world-wide health and social problems.

The ultimate goal of finding happiness is to engage in endeavors which you are good at, love to do, and give you a sense of higher purpose.


## FACING TOUGH DECISIONS

As you move forward to success, you may come to a fork in the road. To keep progressing, you have to make a choice. Otherwise, you are stuck going nowhere. As Yogi Berra said, "When you get to a fork in the road, take it."

Instead of making a decision and taking the first step down

an unknown path—one that could ultimately lead to amazing opportunities and our overall success—we stall for time. Our attention is diverted. We take a nap. We check Facebook. We watch one more episode. Before we know it, years have passed and we haven't budged.

Change can be scary and messy, but worth it. Jump out of an airplane, even if it is a metaphorical one. Take the promotion; go back to school; go on that date; choose to walk away.

I've been there and done that.

I married for the first time when I was 26; 12 years later, it ended in divorce. I won't share any gory details because there are none to share. We were compatible, but we did not belong together.

My family expected me to get an education, find a good job, meet a nice girl, get married, buy a house, settle down, have children, and live happily ever after.

My wife's life had been more chaotic than mine and she didn't envision the same idyllic scene.

Therein lay our struggles. We tried to make things work. Fueled by my Catholic upbringing and the taboo of divorce, I prolonged the inevitable until it became clear that neither one of us would grow and thrive if we remained married.

We had reached a fork in the road. We chose to take different directions.

Life is too short to live with regrets, bitterness, or grudges, and I have nothing but respect for the relationship we once shared. After finally making that tough decision, we were able to move toward lives that were richer and fuller for both of us.

• • •

James, an executive director for a nonprofit association, knew his job might often be subject to the whim of a board of directors. Still, he loved the challenge and made the profession his passion for 23 years.

His passion and sense of purpose was significantly altered when he heard his board members question whether or not the association even needed an executive director. He started to poke around and see what other opportunities might exist.

An executive recruiter told him another association was looking for a director. Over the course of five and a half months, he interviewed his prospective new employer just as hard as they interviewed him. Throughout the interview process, he laid out bold plans that would position the association for success in good times and in bad. There seemed to be a meeting of the minds and after months of the "recruitment dance" he was hired for the new position.

The new position had lots of promise. There was a significant pay increase, opportunities for international travel, and challenge of taking his new association to a level they have never seen before. James jumped in with both feet and began imple-

*In the world of business,*
*the people who*
*are most successful*
*are those who*
*are doing what they love.*

—Warren Buffett

menting his plans.

When he took over, the association was doing well. They were in an excellent financial position and the association members were happy. Soon, James learned that the board of directors hadn't really meant what they said throughout the interview process. The board preferred the status quo and chose not to proceed with the work needed to change and chase new or different ideas.

James was at a fork in the road. He could keep "banging his head against the wall," and "coast" until he was forced out, or he could find something else. After six months, he realized that life was too short, and he resigned.

His passion for association work had reached the "burn out" level.

To abruptly leave a job that provides one's livelihood without a fallback position is not usually advisable. But James had reserve resources, a wife who was employed, and skills that would not leave him unemployed for long.

He set out on a quest to find something completely different. Now he is open to new possibilities. He's floating some ideas which for some may seem preposterous, but is exploring everything, from buying a paint and sip art studio franchise, to becoming a concierge travel consultant. Above all, he says his new trajectory "must be fun and have a good work/life balance."

I can't wait to see where he lands.

• • •

Since you are the one in control, why not keep moving and see where the path takes you? You can always turn around, take the other fork, or abandon the road altogether. Life is too short to stay stuck in a rut.

## Life is Too Short to Worry

My mom, God love her, was the "Queen of Worry." After seeing a commercial about fibromyalgia medication, she was convinced she was suffering from the disease. Her doctor said, "Esther, you watch too much television." One Saturday afternoon she called me from Milwaukee, worried about a tornado that had hit Atlanta. I live in North Carolina; it wasn't about to affect either of us.

In his book *The Gift of Fear,* Gavin de Becker points out people use the words "worry" and "fear" synonymously but they are two entirely different emotions. Fear is the necessary element that alerts us to sudden danger, while worry he characterizes as "a form of self-harassment."

There are things we should fear—like the bear in front of us on the hiking trail. Fear is the emotion that can alert us to danger that lurks ahead. Genuine fear is also what can help us kick into our survival instinct and deal with the bear on our

*I've had a lot of worries in my life, most of which never happened.*

—Mark Twain

path. Worry, on the other hand, is what keeps us from going hiking because we might encounter a bear. De Becker says: "Worry is fear we manufacture."

That worry then manufactures self-limiting beliefs.

Many people worry about and have a fear of flying when in fact, flying is one of the safest forms of travel. In 2017, there were 111 commercial aircraft accidents which accounted for 13 deaths. Comparatively, for the same year, the National Safety Council estimates there were approximately 40,100 deaths in over 5 million motor vehicle accidents. According to flyfright.com, we would have to fly once a day, every day for 22,000 years before we would die in a U.S. commercial airplane accident!

"Yeah, but, it could happen" worriers say. Sure, anything is possible, but highly improbable.

Stop worrying and start living.

## PERSONAL HEALTH AND WELLNESS

If life is indeed too short, we need to be proactive in prolonging this life of ours. If we aren't exercising on a regular basis, our muscles begin to atrophy and eventually our body won't respond or recover as it once did. We don't recall certain things as quickly as we once did. In the long-term, there isn't a lot we can do about our eventual demise. However, we can do plenty of things to slow down the aging process.

Here's the bottom line: there is no fountain of youth and none of us are going to get out of this alive. The key methods in slowing the aging process include: exercising, eating well, taking care of your brain, getting adequate sleep, and taking care of your skin.

Studies suggest that close to three million people die due to lack of, or inadequate, activity. Harvard epidemiologist and researcher, I-Min Lee, concluded that some 5.3 million people die each year because of inactivity.

My conclusion: activity can save your life.

The United States Department of Health and Human Services produced the Physical Activity Guidelines for Americans in 2008. Adults are recommended to accrue 150 minutes per week of moderate intensity, or 75 minutes per week of vigorous intensity aerobic activity. If you can't manage that much, even some activity is better than none at all. For even more extensive benefits, the guidelines suggest increasing those times to 300 minutes or 150 minutes respectively. Further, the recommendation is for the activities to be done in a minimum of 10 minute intervals spread throughout the week. On two or more of those days, we should include muscle-strengthening exercise that involves all major muscle groups.

Surely, we can find 10-42 minutes a day to exercise. Many of us spend that and more watching television.

Life is too short to include all of the confusing guidance which exists to help us maintain optimal health and vitality through nutrition. If there are hundreds of books on anti-aging, there have to be thousands and thousands of books on nutrition. Everywhere you turn, someone has a miraculous diet plan, the cure-all and end-all.

In terms of nutrition, like most things in life, I subscribe to the notion of everything in moderation, including moderation. But the fact is we are facing a health crisis when it comes to weight and nutrition.

According to a 2015 study published in the *Journal of the American Medical Association,* 75% of men and 67% of women older than 25 years are overweight or obese.

The United States Department of Health Human Services (DHS) reports that about half of Americans have one or more preventable diet-related diseases. The diseases include, but are not limited to, type 2 diabetes, cardiovascular, and obesity.

DHS guidelines suggest that adult women take in 1,600-2,400 calories per day and adult men take in 2,000-3,000 calories per day.

Our diets should include fruits, vegetables, lean proteins, whole grains, and healthy oils. Further, we should limit our intake of saturated fats, trans fats, added sugars, and sodium.

In the United States, you may have noticed over the last few years that chain restaurants have begun posting caloric content on their menus. The postings are eye-opening and startling. For years, I thought I was eating smart and healthy, until the calories were posted. At lunch the other day, I saw a lunch item posted with 2,480 calories. For most people, that is a day's-worth of calories, or more! In addition, that lunch entrée probably busted the saturated fat, sugar, and sodium guidelines.

If you want to eat healthy, you need to eat consciously, but first let's have a beer! The rage these days is craft beer. I, like most, enjoy a good craft beer from time to time. A few years ago, as I was leading up to a vacation, I checked the caloric content of one of my favorite craft beers. I found it contained 236 calories! Yes, I needed to limit my intake of my favorite beer and further, the DHS recommends only one or two alcoholic drinks per day.

Why can't eating and drinking be good for you, you ask.

It is, you just need to find the right balance.

Speaking of balance, the brain, along with our eyes, muscles, joints, and vestibular organs are responsible for aiding in balance. Though balance is certainly important in combating the effects of aging, let's look at the broader subject of keeping your brain healthy as a whole.

According to the Cleveland Clinic, a healthy brain is supported by "Six Pillars." The six pillars are physical exercise, food/nutrition, medical health, sleep/relaxation, mental fitness, and social interaction.

Most brain experts say, "Use it or lose it." Though there is mixed information from the experts, playing games may be one way to keep your brain active, supple, and responsive. Crossword puzzles, Sudoku, and computer games such as Tetris are said to help activate the brain in a good way.

Change is good for the brain. Trying new things, traveling to new places, and meeting new people are all good for you. Using your non-dominant hand for tasks is also good exercise for your brain. Think about learning a new language, simply reading a book, or varying your route home to or from work on a regular basis.

Let's sleep on this for a minute. Well, maybe longer than that. According to the National Sleep Foundation, sleep needs vary by age. Newborns need somewhere between 11 and 19 hours of sleep (lucky kids), school age children and teens need around 8-14 hours, adults 6-10 hours, and older adults 5-9 hours.

The following list of outcomes have all been attributed to the lack of or too much sleep.

- Poor Performance
- Executive Function
- Cognition
- Mood
- Learning
- Memory
- Accidents

- Impulse Control
- Suicide
- Divorce
- Mortality
- Stroke
- Obesity

One more way to ensure that you age well is to keep your skin healthy. Your skin is actually the largest organ of your body. It has many functions and has a direct effect on our health. Skin helps us prevent dehydration and keeps out harmful bugs. It helps keep us from danger when it signals us about things like heat, cold, and pain.

The skin also manufactures Vitamin D when it is exposed to sunlight. Vitamin D helps reduce the risk of various diseases, depression, and even helps to enhance weight loss. Vitamin D deficiency can be caused by being indoors too much, living in areas with high pollution, or having darker skin. Oddly enough, sunscreen is also a culprit in Vitamin D deficiency. So it is important to strike a healthy balance between too much sun and too much protection against it.

Like all of the other topics here, there are many common threads. According to *US News & World Report*'s Health Tip, on June 14, 2018, the American Academy of Dermatology suggests the following to protect your skin.

- Seek shade, wear a hat, and apply sunscreen
- Wear sunglasses to limit fine lines around the eyes
- Never use an indoor tanning bed
- Apply moisturizer daily
- Wash your face twice a day
- Don't smoke
- Eat healthy foods and drink plenty of water

- Get a good night's sleep

Maintaining optimal health is one of the keys to helping you live long enough to accomplish all the things you want to experience in life and more.

## "You Can't Just Sit There!"

Larry Walters, a 33-year-old truck driver from Los Angeles, on July 2, 1982, attached more than 40 helium weather balloons to a lawn chair. He had milk jugs full of water for ballast, a large bottle of soda, a pellet gun, a CB radio, an altimeter, and a camera.

Larry planned to soar over L.A. to a height of about 100 feet and take a leisurely sight-seeing flight out to the Mojave dessert. Once the first of his three tethering lines was cut, the other two snapped and Larry soared quickly to nearly 16,000 feet!

He floated into the airspace of the Long Beach, California airport and was spotted by two commercial planes.

Ultimately, he used his pellet gun to deflate some of the balloons but as he descended he got tied up in some power lines and was dangling about five feet in the air. Once he climbed out of his lawn chair and dropped to the ground he was promptly arrested.

When asked why he'd done it, he said, "You can't just sit

there!"

While Larry's adventure is a case study in what NOT to do, it is also a strong illustration of someone boldly seeking the life he wished to lead. Larry always had a dream of learning to fly. In pursuit of that goal, he'd enlisted in the Air Force with the hopes of going to flight school, but that his hopes were dashed because of his poor eyesight.

Even though Larry did a lot of things wrong in his desire to fly, he did two things right—he set a goal and he took action.

• • •

Malcolm Forbes, entrepreneur and publisher of *Forbes* magazine, shared a similar, high-flying spirit though Forbes lived a more lavish lifestyle than Larry Walters. Rather than launching himself in a lawn chair, however, he flew hot air balloons. He owned dozens of balloons, and piloted them across America and around the world. Starting in the early 1980s, he embarked on what he dubbed Friendship Tours, flying balloons to Russia, China, and Turkey.

He knew what he wanted in life and sometimes threw caution to the wind. "Sure, ballooning can be dangerous," he once admitted. But then again, he said, "always keep in mind that the highest accident rate is in the home, especially getting in and out of the bathtub."

And even in death, Forbes epitomizes the thesis of this

chapter. His gravestone is inscribed:"While alive, he lived."
That should be a goal for all of us.

*If you're not having fun,*
*you're doing something wrong.*

—Groucho Marx

# Have Fun! 8

AVING FUN IS NOT the sole key to creating the life of your dreams, but it may be one of the most important factors.

If happiness is rooted in the fond memories, fun is created in the moment. Given that, the more fun we have, the easier it is to be happy.

The definition of fun includes any action, speech, or mood that provides entertainment, amusement, or enjoyment. Entertainment encompasses things like going to a movie, playing a game, or watching college football. Amusement might be found in thrill seeking—riding a roller coaster, or skydiving, or in something as tame as a good joke. We can derive enjoyment from almost anything or any place.

## Why Fun is Important

People who are having fun learn more, remember more, are more productive, happier in their relationships, and enjoy better health. Those are an awful lot of reasons to make fun an integral part of your life.

My grandmother owned Pliszka Hardware which sold nails by the pound, feminine hygiene products, and everything in between. Beyond the store itself was the basement stockroom and warehouse, and a garage that served as an extension of the warehousing operation.

As kids, my siblings and I played hide and seek throughout the store. We played with the merchandise. We pretended to be customers.

In the seventh grade, my grandmother hired me (child labor). That job helped develop my work ethic, provided spending money, and most importantly set me on a course of how to have fun at work.

My responsibilities were wide-ranging. When a customer picked a specific color of paint, like a scientist in a laboratory, I would carefully measure and add the various tints in the specified quantity to produce their chosen color. Sometimes I would pretend that the addition or omission of a particular amount of tint would result in destruction of the world. High stakes! I learned how to cut glass to size, scoring the glass just so and then tapping it just right to get a good clean break. Like mixing paint, I imagined that unless I cut it just right, it would come crashing down on me.

Making my job a game made it fun.


## GREATER RETENTION

Judy Willis, in her book, *Research Based Strategies to Ignite Student Learning: Insights from a Neurologist and Classroom Teacher*, wrote, "When a lesson starts with humor, there is more alerting, and the subsequent information is attached to the positive emotional event as an event or flashbulb memory."

My recollection of college economics classes is slim at best, with the exception of the utility theory of economics. The utility theory stands out as a flashbulb memory.

If you look up utility theory on businessdictionary.com you'll see it defined as what happens when: "...the rational consumer will not spend money on the additional unit of good or service unless its marginal utility is at least equal to or greater than that of a unit of another good or service..."

My professor started with a definition similar to the one above. Then he told us to imagine we were hungry college students with limited spending power—not too much of a stretch. Then he had us imagine we had enough money to buy one, two, three, or more cheeseburgers.

One cheeseburger, he said, might marginally satisfy our ravenous hunger. A second one might be even more satisfying, but a third one not so much. With that description, we quickly understood that there is a limit to how much is enough and how much we would be willing to shell out for getting enough. Thus, the utility theory of economics "in a bun" as opposed to a nutshell.

To this day, I remember the utility theory because the professor used an entertaining description of the theory and it stuck with me.

## GREATER PRODUCTIVITY AND CREATIVITY

If you have to work, I hope you are doing something you love, or at the very least something you enjoy. Your boss should hope so too because fun has a direct correlation to productivity.

A recent study by the Social Market Foundation and the University of Warwick found 12-20% increases in productivity when employees were shown a 10-minute comedy clip, or offered snacks. Such an increase is extraordinary given that a productivity jump of just 3% of Gross Domestic Product is considered significant.

Conversely, a lack of fun can be counter productive, and leads to stress in the workplace. According to Dr. Robert Pearl, M.D., one-third of U.S. workers felt extremely stressed at work (*Forbes* magazine, October 9, 2014). Stress is estimated to cost businesses about $300 billion per year in absenteeism, diminished productivity, and on-the-job accidents.

Imagine that if minimizing stress through the addition of fun in the workplace would produce results in line with the Warwick study—the resulting gains would be worth $36-60 billion!

Stuart Brown, M.D., founder of the National Institute for Play says, "All sorts of creative new connections are made when you're playing that otherwise would never be made." Once unheard of in corporate America, innovative companies, such as Avidxchange, LinkedIn, Google, Zappos, and Facebook, are transforming the workplace from the sterile offices and cubicles of the past to wide-open play oriented workplaces. Giant slides, volley ball courts, free cafeterias, bowling alleys, foosball, and ping pong tables adorn their campuses. What's more, employees are encouraged to use them "on company time."

These companies have found when their employees work as hard as they play, they stay engaged, and this increases their productivity and creativity.

• • •

While in high school, four friends and I were the "Saturday Night Gang" at the local bakery. At the bakery, there was no big slide, ping pong, or foosball table, but we had fun and were more productive to boot.

At about 10:00 p.m. each Saturday night we reported to Arnie, the owner of the bakery. Along with the five of us high school guys was Earl, an elderly gentleman whose job was to fry the donuts.

Arnie usually left after the dough was made and he was sure we knew what had to be accomplished during our shift. Once Earl finished frying the donuts, he left, too, and then it was just us kids running the operation.

The work from this point wasn't too difficult. It mostly consisted of frosting and filling the donuts and proofing and baking the bread. There wasn't too much we could screw up, but there was plenty of ways we could have fun.

Inevitably a pan of rolls or bread would get dropped and ruined, or there would be some dough that wasn't needed. That made for some great dough fights. It made for some unusually shaped (use your imagination) or oversized (again use your imagination) baked goods.

We soon discovered that it only took two of us to "man" the ovens so we developed a system where two of us worked the ovens while two of us hung out (or napped) on the flour sacks for about an hour. The fifth man frosted and filled donuts. Then we rotated, so everyone had a chance for free time.

Sometimes, people leaving the local bars would stop by wanting to barter a six pack of beer for some fresh baked goods. I can neither confirm nor deny that those transactions occurred.

From time to time, night shift patrol officers would show up at the back door. (Imagine that, police at a donut shop!) Though we had a ton of fun, we also produced pretty good tasting baked goods, on time, every weekend.

• • •

We have all seen landscapers wearing 3M dust masks over their mouths and noses while they blow our leaves to kingdom come. But did you know that those masks came about when the company was actually developing new materials to be used in molded, nonwoven women's brassieres?

In the 1960s, an employee is alleged to have pulled a sophomoric and misogynistic prank: he put one of the bra cups over his face. With that, a new product was born.

The employee was having fun, probably trying to alleviate the tedium of his day, and stumbled upon an invention that ultimately made his company millions of dollars. I don't know if 3M makes bra cups, but I do know they have a significant market share in the respiratory protection market.

• • •

Remember the movie *Mary Poppins* and the song "A Spoonful of Sugar"? If you are like me, you might recall it as a song about how to get a child to take his medicine, but we'd be wrong. The song is actually about how you can find an element of fun in even the worst tasks. When you approach any job with fun in mind, it becomes a "piece of cake."

As we navigate life, there will be plenty of things we must do that are not particularly fun. But if we consciously choose to infuse them with fun, these things become more bearable and, in time, perhaps even enjoyable.

When our lives are more filled with fun—are sweeter—we can more easily handle the uncomfortable or the unforeseen.

In the diagram below, the black dots are the same size, but the one in the smaller gray circle appears larger because it represents a great proportion of the whole.

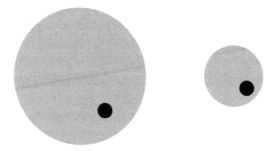

Suppose the gray circles were two glasses filled with water and the black dots were drops of something incredibly bitter. In which glass would the unappealing taste be less noticeable?

The answer, of course, is the larger glass.

When you make your life a big container, filled with good experiences and pleasant relationships, you can better absorb life's unpleasantness.

When our glasses are small and not filled with sweetness, when our lives are devoid of pleasure, fun, and play, bad things can happen.

Dr. Brown has closely studied individuals whose lives have taken drastic turns for the worse due to the lack of fun and play in their lives. One such case study focused on Charles Whitman who, on August 1, 1966, killed 16 people and wounded 31, in Austin, Texas. Whitman, who tested at age 6 with an IQ of 139, grew up in a very strict and regimented household.

Dr. Brown found similar causal correlations between play-deprived children and violent criminals. His research shows that play is directly correlated to positive human development.

Brown is a strong advocate for continuing play into adulthood. And surprisingly, he defines the opposite of play—not as work as you might think—but as depression.

This is important: *play helps minimize depression.*

Similarly, Dr. Bruce Charlton, a British doctor and professor of psychology, theorizes that an adult who maintains psychological neoteny (juvenile characteristics) is better equipped to cope with our dynamic contemporary society. Charlton sees increased neoteny in more highly educated individuals. Those who can adapt a more youthful mindset tend to be more open to new ideas, and can better cope with rapid change and uncertainty.

*You can be childlike
without being childish.
A child always wants to have fun.
Ask yourself, 'Am I having fun?'*

—Christopher Meloni

## ENHANCED RELATIONSHIPS

Think about all of the various relationships in your life. Aren't the best ones filled with fun? Maybe you play cards, golf, or trivia with this group. Maybe you are in a church or social group. I bet the ones where you have fun are the best ones.

Sure, each group may have its curmudgeon, but for the most part, you have fun and if you really looked at the group, it is because you share a similar sense of humor and have similar views on life.

Professor Jeffrey Hall, a communications researcher at the University of Kansas. found that sharing a similar sense of humor and playfulness can be a make or break a relationship between partners, children, friends, and family. It's not just being funny or humorous, it is about sharing a similar sense of humor that leads to continued compatibility.

My wife and I know two couples who have been married more than 50 years and their vitality and zest for life are unmatched. They are in, or approaching, their 80s and they still play golf, travel, exercise, read, and enjoy a wide social network. Both these couples seem to complete each other. They are full of praise and respect for their spouses. Sure, they laugh and can sarcastically describe each other's weaknesses, but they are quick to maintain the fun in their relationships. It's part of what keeps them strong.

## BETTER HEALTH

Modern culture tends to frown on adults engaging in play, unless it is of a competitive nature. However, having fun can lead to better health.

Traditionally, doctors are taught that healthy is absence of disease, or in medical terminology—within normal limits (WNL). Author of *Why Normal Isn't Healthy*, Dr. Bowen F. White, takes an interesting view of what *is* healthy. He turns the traditional definition on its head and defines healthy as "the ability to work, to love, to play, and to think soundly."

White's definition of healthy includes a person with disease (e.g., cancer, or hypertension); likewise, a person free of disease can be unhealthy if he is unable to work, live, love, or think soundly. His definition builds on that of British-American anthropologist Ashley Montagu who maintained that keeping in touch with our inner child allows us to remain vital and thrive.

• • •

No one can deny that actor and comedian George Burns was a fun guy. While he maintained a regimen of swimming, walking, and exercise until very late in life, *Cigar Aficionado* reported that Burns smoked cigars for at least 70 years, 10-15 cigars on any given day! He lived to be 100.

Burns' was discovered singing harmonies with co-workers at a candy factory when he was just seven years old. From that

*The idea is to die young*
*as late as possible.*

—Ashley Montagu

point on, he continued working in show business for more than nine decades.

Undoubtedly, working in a business of "fun" played a role in his longevity. So, too, did his propensity for enjoying life—and cigars—on a daily basis.

• • •

After traveling to Russia, Norman Cousins, the editor of *The Saturday Review,* was diagnosed with ankylosing spondylitis, a degenerative disease that left him in constant pain. Though his doctor said he had less than a year to live, Cousins disagreed. He thought the disease was stress-related. He checked himself out of the hospital and into a nearby hotel.

There he received high doses of Vitamin C and watched a treasure trove of funny films. Cousins found that ten minutes of deep laughter relieved his pain and allowed him about two hours of sleep. When his pain returned, he repeated the laughter therapy. Within six months he was back on his feet. In two years he returned to work. His doctor was amazed.

Was he cured, was the original diagnosis wrong, or was it placebo affect? Did it matter? Cousins lived 26 years past his doctor's initial prognosis.

• • •

In 1971, Patch Adams, physician and clown, founded the

Gesundheit! Institute. (Robin Williams portrayed him in a semi-biographical film.) When Adams was young, he experienced bullying and became suicidal. At 18 years old, Adams decided to be happy and never have another bad day. "You don't kill yourself, stupid; you make revolution."

The Gesundheit! Institute, a non-profit healthcare organization, was founded on the belief that one cannot separate the health of the individual from the health of the family, the community, the society, and the world. Its mission is to reframe the concept of 'hospital.' Though there is a lack of empirical data as to the effectiveness of Adams' practice, he continues to dedicate his life to bring humor and healing to the masses around the world at little to no cost to the patient.


## LET'S GO PLAY

It's hard to talk about fun without mentioning the word play. According to the National Institute for Play, there are several types of play and they work together to improve brain function and ultimately ensure our survival:

1. ATTUNEMENT PLAY: This type of play is used when getting used to, or accustomed to, something new. This might be the play of a young child acclimating herself to the new world in which she lives. This play helps babies organize emotional

control. Even adults engage in attunement play. The audiophile who buys a new piece of stereo equipment "plays" with the equipment as he becomes attuned to his new device.

2. BODY PLAY AND MOVEMENT: This play is discovering and understanding human movement. Think of the joy of a child jumping on a bed. He is discovering how to move his body and at the same time he is discovering gravity. Adults engage in body play and movement by dancing, swimming, running, and sex.

3. OBJECT PLAY: Play associated with manipulating various objects begins when a child engages with simple things like shaking a rattle, or gnawing on a teething ring. As we mature, most engage in more complex object play that helps develop problem solving skills. It becomes more sophisticated over time and might be used while we engage in hobbies such as woodworking or needlepoint.

4. SOCIAL PLAY: This type of play occurs when we interact with others. This play progresses from very rudimentary actions such as a simple game of peek-a-boo, to elaborate interactions and shenanigans among the best of friends. Social play is one of the most prevalent forms of play and is a key to continued growth and learning in the individual.

5. IMAGINATIVE AND PRETEND PLAY: This play, associated with finding one's own sense of mind, helps develop coping skills and trust. It also increases our capacity for innovation and creativity. Imaginative play is best described as role playing, pretending to be a fireman, policeman, pirate, school teacher, or some other character.

6. STORYTELLING OR NARRATIVE PLAY: According to the National Institute for Play, this is the way most kids like to learn and is associated with telling a story or hearing a narrative, e.g., a parent telling a child: "When I was your age…" In business, storyboards are often used to illustrate processes and procedures.

7. CREATIVE PLAY: Accessing fantasy and imagination (imagining we are somewhere else or doing something else) helps us become more innovative and creative while coping with variation in the patterns of life.

## DON'T TAKE YOURSELF SO SERIOUSLY

Rosamund Stone Zander and Benjamin Zander, in their book, *The Art of Possibility*, tell everyone, "Don't take yourself so goddamn seriously." (Their words, not mine!)

Not taking yourself too seriously is a gateway to having fun and gives you license to be who you are and not someone you think others want you to be. Being a bit less serious may make you more approachable to others which may help you open new horizons of opportunity.

During the 2012 Democratic National Convention in Charlotte, North Carolina, law enforcement officers came from other towns to help with various policing duties, including directing traffic.

As two officers from Georgia directed uptown traffic the Saturday before the convention began, they started mimicking pedestrians and others passing through their intersection. When a police equestrian unit passed, the officers acted as if they too were riding horses. They cooed at sleeping babies in strollers. Before long, camera crews were filming them and their antics were broadcast on national television.

That intersection also had cameras with direct feed to the police emergency operations center. The chief of police observed what was going on and commanded the officer in charge to record the two Georgia policemen. Everyone in the command center assumed those officers were in trouble. Not so. The chief saw their behavior as a positive example of how approachable police could be. He asked for the video because he wanted to make sure the officers from Georgia had a record of their community-building exploits.

# CONCLUSION

I wish you godspeed as you pursue the life of your dreams, and I hope these seven guidelines help you reach your destination!

1. Remember you are in control; you're the one deciding what it is you want and how you're going to get it.

2. Listen to my parents and believe that above all, "You can!"

3. Like Captain Kirk, BOLDLY go toward your dreams!

4. Define your values and be true to them so that your life is in balance.

5. Face it, you don't know everything. Everyone is smarter than you about something—don't be afraid to ask for help.

6. Stop waiting for the right moment. Get going now! Tomorrow is not guaranteed.

7. Whatever you do, have *fun!*

And like shampoo bottle directions advise: *Lather, Rinse, Repeat* do likewise with this book: *Read, Implement, Re-read!*

# ACKNOWLEDGEMENTS

I want to thank all my friends, who heard me say more than once, "I can't, I'm working on my book." Thank you for your patience and understanding while we missed many a day on, under, or over the lake.

Gratitude to my brother Wally, for giving me an "A" when I took on my various life adventures, and to my sisters, Shirley and Ann, for looking after their little brother and for dressing him up as a girl to see if Mom would recognize me when I rang the doorbell. (They say, "what doesn't kill you, makes you stronger.") To John H. Olson, Ph.D., who taught me the meaning of being BOLD and who motivated me to chase the life of my dreams. To Andrew John Halstead, the graduate school roommate I thought I would most dislike (while he thought the same of me), whose life-long friendship I treasure. For the late Mitch Byrd, who taught me to laugh like there was no tomorrow. To Jay McKinstry whose electronic calendar invite pushed me to get off my duff and finally write this book. To all of the people I have ever met, befriended, pissed-off, or encountered along the way: without you, my life would be far less rich and this book would not have been possible.

Thanks to Wanda Beilenson for the creative book title.

Most of all, thanks to Leslie Rindoks, my editor, without whom this book would never have come into existence. She proved the thesis of Chapter 6, that everyone is smarter than you about something. Because of Leslie, I am a much better writer and perhaps just a tad bit more organized in my writing style. Her guidance and tutelage was invaluable.

# APPENDICES

## AFFIRMATIONS

On the lines below, write short, *positive* phrases that will remind you of things you would like to bring into your life; write them as if they have already happened. ("I am punctual and on-time; I am happy and positive; I am pursuing my education in…") There is no limit to the number of affirmations you may make, but you should be able to read your list aloud in no more than a minute or two. Repeat your statements once or twice a day (morning and night). Over the first few weeks, edit the statements to fit your actual desires. Many of these statements might stay on your list forever, while others might cease to be necessary. Continue the affirmation process for the rest of your life.

- _____
  _____

- _____
  _____

- _____
  _____

- _____
  _____

- _____
  _____

- _____
  _____

Use these worksheets for your life audit.

## LIFE ASPECT:

| Going Well | Needs Improvement |
|---|---|

10   9   8   7   6   5   4   3   2   1

## LIFE ASPECT:

| Going Well | Needs Improvement |
|---|---|

10   9   8   7   6   5   4   3   2   1

# Time Inventory

Use the table below to track your week. Where and how are you spending your time? Could you eliminate or streamline some of your activities to spend time on endeavors that will help you reach that life of your dreams?

| Hours Spent Per Day | | | | | | | |
|---|---|---|---|---|---|---|---|
| ACTIVITY | Mon. | Tue. | Wed. | Thurs. | Fri. | Sat. | Sun. |
| Sleeping | | | | | | | |
| Grooming | | | | | | | |
| Commuting | | | | | | | |
| Working | | | | | | | |
| Television | | | | | | | |
| Internet | | | | | | | |
| Meal Prep. | | | | | | | |
| Eating | | | | | | | |
| Exercising | | | | | | | |
| Hobbies | | | | | | | |
| Self-Improvement | | | | | | | |
| Chores | | | | | | | |
| Child Care | | | | | | | |
| Other: | | | | | | | |
| Other: | | | | | | | |

# ADDITIONAL READING

Below is a list of books, in no particular order, that I have found helpful along the way. In them I found some great ideas that helped me move forward, perhaps you will too.

- *The 7 Habits of Highly Effective People*, Stephen R. Covey
- *Ignite the Third Factor*, Dr. Peter Jensen
- *The Art of Possibility: Transforming Professional and Personal Life*, Rosamund Stone Zander, Benjamin Zander
- *Top Performer: A Bold Approach to Sales and Service*, Stephen C. Lundin
- *The Road Less Traveled*, M. Scott Peck, M.D.
- *The Secret*, Rhonda Byrne
- *North to the Pole*, Will Steger and Paul Schurke
- *Think and Grow Rich*, Napoleon Hill
- *Keys to Success, The 17 Principles of Personal Achievement*, Napoleon Hill
- *The One Minute Manager Meets the Monkey*, Kenneth Blanchard and William Oncken, Jr.
- *Who Moved My Cheese?: An Amazing Way to Deal with Change in Your Work and in Your Life*, Spencer Johnson, M.D.
- *The Four Agreements*, Don Miguel Ruiz

## About the Author

Dan Pliszka describes himself as a respectfully irreverent and enthusiastic public speaker, thinker, traveler, observer, smart-ass, and wine enthusiast. His life adventures include, but are not limited to: traveling around the world, racing Porsches, skydiving, skiing, and speaking to groups large and small.

Visit www.dpgreatlife.com for more information.